Living Life Without a Mask
Authentically and Unapologetically You!

Empowerment Manual & Workbook

Dr. Cassundra White-Elliott

This manual is the property of _____.
Send a text or email to _____ if found.

clfpublishing.org
909.315.3161

*All included scriptures are from the
New International Version (NIV) of the Holy Bible.*

Copyright © 2023 by Cassundra White-Elliott.

All rights reserved. No portion of this book may be reproduced, stored in a retrieval system, or transmitted by any form or any means electronically, photocopied, recorded, or any other except for brief quotations in printed reviews, without the prior permission of the publisher.

Cover design by Senir Design. Contact info: info@senirdesign.com

ISBN #978-1-945102-97-4

Dedication

For all who dare to live unapologetically as their authentic self.

Contents

Guidelines for Individual Users & Group Leaders	ix
Introduction	11

Chapter One: *Understanding Self* 15

Integrity	20
Intelligence	33
Wisdom	38
Compassion	47
Humility	59
Patience	67
Dedication	79
Discipline	86
Contentment	95

Chapter Two: *Why the Mask?* 103

Avoiding Scrutiny and Judgment	105
Shielding Insecurities	106
Shame & Embarrassment	109
Regret	120
Disappointment	126
Iniquity	135
Jealousy	144
Envy	152
Covetousness	161

Chapter Three: *Remove the Mask* 169

Why be Authentic?	171
- Trust and Respect	172
- Integrity	173
- Ability to deal with problems	173

- Realizing potential	175
- Confidence and self-esteem	176
- Less stress	177
Being Authentic in Different Roles	178
How to Be Authentic	178
- Live by Your Values	178
- Identify the Gap	180
- Live with Integrity	181
- Communicate Honestly	185
- Don't Make Assumptions	189
- Develop Self-Confidence	192
- Manage Your Emotions	196

Chapter Four: *Developing Self-Assuredness* — 201

Dealing with Insecurities and the Fear of Judgment	203
- Talk to a Spiritual Counselor	204
- Acknowledge the Role of Insecurity in Daily Life	207
- Fully Assess the Source of Insecurity	209
- Practice Unconditional Self-Compassion	209
- Retrain Yourself	213
- Openly Communicate Your Insecurity Concerns	215
- Build a Strong Support Network	218
- Focus on the Positives	219
- Take Care of Your Physical Health	221
- Accept Your Limitations & Celebrate Your Differences	222
- Aim for Progress, Not Perfection	223
Final Thoughts on Insecurity	224

References	226
About the Author	228
Gift of Salvation	229
Additional Titles by Author	232

Guidelines for *Without a Mask* Empowerment Manual & Workbook

For the Individual User
- Be sure to read the *Introduction* to gain a clear understanding of the manual's purpose.
- Before each session, go to the Lord in prayer, so your mind can be clear of all distractions. As you go through this journey of self-improvement with the intent of discovering and revealing your authentic self, you want to embark upon this journey with a clear mind.
- Be sure to complete each section in order along with all corresponding exercises to maximize the overall experience and outcome. Take your time, so you can properly absorb the heart of each section into your countenance and spirit. Remember, transforming your life should not be viewed as a fast-paced marathon but rather as a cross country trek.

For Group Leaders
- Thank you for taking on the privilege of ushering others into their authentic selves! You are doing a great work for the Lord.
- Be sure to read the *Introduction* to gain a clear understanding of the manual's purpose.
- Begin each session with an opening prayer. Then, address any follow-up questions from the prior lesson before engaging in the new lesson. This will give the class members an opportunity to gain clarity any points that may have been vague, misunderstood, or overlooked. Also, consider having make-up sessions for anyone who may have missed a session in order to keep them on a smooth path to self-betterment.
- At the beginning of each session (after the prayer), provide a short overview of the lesson's topic, i.e. integrity.
- Then, from the list of scripture for the lesson, choose two or three verses to focus a brief discussion on. Do not attempt to cover the entire list. The focus of the sessions should be the Group Discussion sections of the manual. Please note- the Personal Reflections are private for the user and are not intended for open discussion.
- When devising a course calendar, be consistent and take into consideration holidays and other events, such as church events, that may impact the convening of the class.
- At the completion of all of the lessons in the manual, consider offering a certificate to the attendees.

This manual can be completed over a non-specified length of time. However, a 26-week period is suggested.
See the suggested schedule below.

Chapter One (Nine Lessons)
Session One- *Integrity*
Session Two- *Intelligence*
Session Three- *Wisdom*
Session Four- *Compassion*
Session Five- *Humility*
Session Six- *Patience*
Session Seven- *Dedication*
Session Eight- *Discipline*
Session Nine- *Contentment*

Chapter Two (Seven Lessons)
Session Ten- *Shame & Embarrassment*
Session Eleven- *Regret*
Session Twelve- *Disappointment*
Session Thirteen- *Iniquity*
Session Fourteen- *Jealousy*
Session Fifteen- *Envy*
Session Sixteen- *Covetousness*

Chapter Three (Five Lessons)
Session Seventeen – Group Discussion pg. 184
Session Eighteen - Group Discussion pg. 187
Session Nineteen - Group Discussion pg. 190
Session Twenty - Group Discussion pg. 193
Session Twenty-One - Group Discussion pg. 199

Chapter Four (Five Lessons)
Session Twenty-Two - Group Discussion pg. 212
Session Twenty-Three - Group Discussion pg. 214
Session Twenty-Four - Group Discussion pg. 217
Session Twenty-Five - Group Discussion pg. 220
Session Twenty-Six - Group Discussion pg. 221

Introduction

This book was designed with honesty in mind, honesty about your true identity (your true character makeup). This workbook will guide you step by step as you take an in-depth look within and examine yourself with a critical lens. Your objective here is to learn how to be authentic and to be unapologetic about who you are.

Authenticity means you are true to your personality, values, and spirit, regardless of the pressure you are under to act otherwise. You are honest with yourself and with others, and you take responsibility for your mistakes. Your values, ideals, and actions all align. As a result, you come across as genuine, and you are willing to accept the consequences of being true to what you consider to be right.

Consider this:

Your parents and siblings know you pretty well because they were with you as you grew up, when your character was being developed. Of course, you are not the exact same person you were when you were younger, but many of the same personality traits you embodied as a young person are still evident within you today. Regardless of how well your parents and siblings know you, they do not know you through and through. Even your best friend(s) and your mate does not know you through and through. There are always components of yourself that you do not share with others.

The only person who knows the true totality of your personality and character is you. And, of course, God knows who you are. After all, He is the omniscient creator who knows your unique design and your capabilities. *"Before I formed you in the womb I knew you, before you were born I set you apart"* (Jeremiah 1:5, NIV).

As you complete the exercises in this workbook, dare to be completely transparent with yourself. You may be thinking, *I'm always honest with myself.* The reality is some of us have been wearing a mask so long that we have come to believe we are actually the person we created in our mind. But are we really that person, or is there another person that exists underneath?

The exercises in this book will assist in uncovering your authentic self, one you should love and embrace. If you uncover someone you really don't care to be, you will discover how you can change yourself to become someone you can be proud of and really are rather than someone you are/have been pretending to be.

As we explore ourselves to uncover our authentic self, we may find that we shift who we are depending on who we are surrounded by from one setting to the next. The shift we make as we navigate various arenas could simply display a different part of our total persona, or it could be a changing of masks (identities) to display whom we aspire or are pretending to be.

When we were children, we put on the mask of a "good" child when in reality, we may have been hellraisers. On our job, we wear the mask of being the qualified, attentive employee when in reality, we may be lazy wretches. Spouses present themselves as loving, dedicated partners when they may be on the prowl for their next victim to ensnare with their charm.

The reality is we all wear a mask to a lesser or greater degree. And, we need to ask ourselves why. What is it we are trying to keep hidden? What is it we don't want people to see or know about us? What is it we believe others will not accept about us? What is it that sets us apart from others that we believe causes us to not fit in with the crowd? Why do we need to fit in with the masses? If we accept our authentic self and only adhere to God's expectations, others will begin to accept our authentic self, too.

So, stop hiding.

Come from behind the mask(s).

Being authentic and unapologetic about who you are means not having to fit into someone's idea of who you should be. As a believer, you should allow the Word of God to dictate the characteristics you behold.

We only have one life to live, and we want to be our best self … in our God-given glory!

Chapter One
Understanding Self: Who Am I

Chapter One
Understanding Self: Who Am I?

Your personality is comprised of character traits that set you apart from others and cause you to be a unique individual. Personality traits reflect your pattern of thoughts, feelings, and behaviors and help others understand who you are personally and professionally because the traits express your true nature.

There are many character traits that you may presently embody or develop (if you aspire to), such as integrity, intelligence, wisdom, compassion, humility, patience, dedication, discipline, and contentment. Before even reading the remainder of this chapter, think about positive character traits you believe you embody. List them here and feel free to include any that have not yet been mentioned. Remember, no one is going to see this list other than you, so be completely honest with yourself.

1. _____
2. _____
3. _____
4. _____
5. _____
6. _____
7. _____
8. _____
9. _____
10. _____

Dr. C. White-Elliott

As you pondered the character traits you believe you currently possess, you may have considered a few traits you desire to have but either do not or they have only been weakly developed. List those here:

1. _____
2. _____
3. _____
4. _____
5. _____
6. _____
7. _____
8. _____
9. _____
10. _____

Now, form a list of personality traits you do not care to embody due to their harmful nature (either to yourself or others) but presently do.

1. _____
2. _____
3. _____
4. _____
5. _____
6. _____
7. _____
8. _____
9. _____

10. _____

Continue to survey these three lists as you read this chapter and complete the included exercises. The lists will serve as a reminder about who you currently are and where you would like to be as you transition from your current state to your authentic self.

Integrity
(trustworthiness)

Integrity is the practice of being honest and showing a consistent and uncompromising adherence to strong moral and ethical principles and values (*Oxford Living Dictionaries*, 2023); (*Cambridge Dictionary*, 2023); (Killinger, 2010). In ethics, integrity is regarded as the honesty and truthfulness or earnestness of one's actions. Integrity can stand in opposition to hypocrisy (the practice of feigning to be what one is not) (Lucaites, Condit, & Caudill, 1999). It regards internal consistency as a virtue, and suggests that people who hold apparently conflicting values should account for the discrepancy or seek to alter the conflicting values.

In ethics, a person is said to possess the virtue of integrity if the person's actions are based upon an internally consistent framework of principles, such as a belief system (MacCallum, 1993); (Pillai, 2011). A person has ethical integrity to the extent that the person's actions, beliefs, methods, measures, and principles are all consistent with a well-integrated core group of values. A person must, therefore, be flexible and willing to adjust these values to maintain consistency when these values are challenged—such as when an expected result is not congruent with all observed outcomes. Because such flexibility is a form of accountability, it is regarded as a moral responsibility as well as a virtue. A person's value system (or moral compass) provides a framework within which the person acts in ways that are consistent and expected. The concept of integrity implies a wholeness - a comprehensive set of beliefs often referred to as a worldview or personal belief system that shapes his/her view from which to operate. This concept of wholeness emphasizes honesty and authenticity, requiring that one act at all times in accordance with one's worldview/belief system.

Viewing integrity through a Christian lens:

Honesty is marked as being free from deceit or untruthfulness, being sincere. The Christian life should be one marked with integrity and honesty, yet because we all sin and find it easy to do so, honesty is something we must work hard at! An honest life is important on so many levels from relationships with spouses and children, at our workplace, and interacting with our neighbors. Matthew 7:16 tells us that we are known by our fruit. Let us be examples of a God of truth and life by living lives of integrity and truthfulness. Read the below Bible verses on honesty and remember God's blessings on those who live by truthful words and actions! (Strong's Online Concordance, 2023)

All throughout scripture, we can identify the importance of integrity. In the sinful world we live in today, it is obvious that our integrity is imperfect. Perfect integrity can be found in Jesus, and through Him, we are able to aim towards true integrity for ourselves.

Use these Bible verses for a better understanding of integrity. Read each verse. Then, rewrite it in your own words. Doing so will assist in understanding the concept of integrity better.

Deuteronomy 9:5 (NIV)
"It is not because of your righteousness or your integrity that you are going in to take possession of their land; but on account of the wickedness of these nations, the LORD your God will drive them out before you, to accomplish what he swore to your fathers, to Abraham, Isaac and Jacob."

_____

_____

_____

I Kings 9:4 (NIV)
"As for you, if you walk before me faithfully with integrity of heart and uprightness, as David your father did, and do all I command and observe my decrees and laws."

_____

_____

_____

I Chronicles 29:17 (NIV)
"I know, my God, that you test the heart and are pleased with integrity. All these things I have given willingly and with honest intent. And now I have seen with joy how willingly your people who are here have given to you."

_____

_____

_____

Job 2:3 (NIV)
"Then the LORD said to Satan, 'Have you considered my servant Job? There is no one on earth like him; he is blameless and upright, a man who fears God and shuns evil. And he still maintains his integrity, though you incited me against him to ruin him without any reason'."

_____

_____

_____

Job 2:9 (NIV)
"His wife said to him, 'Are you still maintaining your integrity? Curse God and die!'"

___

___

___

Job 6:29 (NIV)
"Relent, do not be unjust; reconsider, for my integrity is at stake."

___

___

___

Job 27:5 (NIV)
"I will never admit you are in the right; till I die, I will not deny my integrity."

___

___

___

Psalm 7:8 (NIV)
"Let the LORD judge the peoples. Vindicate me, LORD, according to my righteousness, according to my integrity, O Most High."

___

___

___

Psalm 25:21 (NIV)

"May integrity and uprightness protect me, because my hope, LORD, is in you."

_____

_____

_____

Psalm 41:12 (NIV)

"Because of my integrity you uphold me and set me in your presence forever."

_____

_____

_____

Psalm 78:72 (NIV)

"And David shepherded them with integrity of heart; with skillful hands he led them."

_____

_____

_____

Proverbs 10:9 (NIV)

"Whoever walks in integrity walks securely, but whoever takes crooked paths will be found out."

Proverbs 11:3 (NIV)
"The integrity of the upright guides them, but the unfaithful are destroyed by their duplicity."

Proverbs 13:6 (NIV)
"Righteousness guards the person of integrity, but wickedness overthrows the sinner."

Proverbs 29:10 (NIV)
"The bloodthirsty hate a person of integrity and seek to kill the upright."

Isaiah 45:23 (NIV)
"By myself I have sworn, my mouth has uttered in all integrity a word that will not be revoked: Before me every knee will bow; by me every tongue will swear."

_____

_____

Isaiah 59:4 (NIV)
"No one calls for justice; no one pleads a case with integrity. They rely on empty arguments, they utter lies; they conceive trouble and give birth to evil."

_____

_____

Matthew 22:16 (NIV)
"They sent their disciples to him along with the Herodians. 'Teacher,' they said, 'we know that you are a man of integrity and that you teach the way of God in accordance with the truth. You aren't swayed by others, because you pay no attention to who they are'."

_____

_____

Mark 12:14 (NIV)
"They came to him and said, 'Teacher, we know that you are a man of integrity. You aren't swayed by others, because you pay no attention to who they are; but you teach the way of God in accordance with the truth. Is it right to pay the imperial tax to Caesar or not?'"

_____
_____
_____

II Corinthians 1:12 (NIV)
"Now this is our boast: Our conscience testifies that we have conducted ourselves in the world, and especially in our relations with you, with integrity and godly sincerity. We have done so, relying not on worldly wisdom but on God's grace."

_____
_____
_____

Titus 2:7 (NIV)
"In everything set them an example by doing what is good. In your teaching show integrity, seriousness."

_____
_____
_____

Personal Reflection

Think of a time when your integrity was challenged. Share the experience below and include how you responded in the situation.

_____
_____
_____
_____
_____
_____
_____
_____
_____
_____
_____
_____
_____

Were you pleased with your response at the time? Why or why not?

_____
_____
_____
_____
_____

Looking back, are you still pleased with your response today? Why or why not? If not, what would you do differently if you were presented the same challenge again?

_____
_____
_____
_____
_____
_____

Group Discussion

Read the story of David and Bathsheba (II Samuel 11:1-27, NIV) and discuss David's level of integrity. Then, share what David should have done differently in order to act in a manner that is pleasing to God, demonstrating himself as a man of integrity.

> *In the spring, at the time when kings go off to war, David sent Joab out with the king's men and the whole Israelite army. They destroyed the Ammonites and besieged Rabbah. But David remained in Jerusalem. ² One evening David got up from his bed and walked around on the roof of the palace. From the roof he saw a woman bathing. The woman was very beautiful, ³ and David sent someone to find out about her. The man said, "She is Bathsheba, the daughter of Eliam and the wife of Uriah the Hittite." ⁴ Then David sent messengers to get her. She came to him, and he slept with her. (Now she was purifying herself from her monthly uncleanness.) Then she went back home. ⁵ The woman conceived and sent word to David, saying, "I am pregnant." ⁶ So David sent this word to Joab: "Send me Uriah the Hittite." And Joab sent him*

to David. ⁷ *When Uriah came to him, David asked him how Joab was,* how the soldiers were and how the war was going. ⁸ Then David said *to Uriah, "Go down to your house and wash your feet." So Uriah left the palace, and a gift from the king was sent after him.* ⁹ *But Uriah slept at the entrance to the palace with all his master's servants and did not go down to his house.* ¹⁰ *David was told, "Uriah did not go home." So he asked Uriah, "Haven't you just come from a military campaign? Why didn't you go home?"* ¹¹ *Uriah said to David, "The ark and Israel and Judah are staying in tents, and my commander Joab and my lord's men are camped in the open country. How could I go to my house to eat and drink and make love to my wife? As surely as you live, I will not do such a thing!"* ¹² *Then David said to him, "Stay here one more day, and tomorrow I will send you back." So Uriah remained in Jerusalem that day and the next.* ¹³ *At David's invitation, he ate and drank with him, and David made him drunk. But in the evening Uriah went out to sleep on his mat among his master's servants; he did not go home.* ¹⁴ *In the morning David wrote a letter to Joab and sent it with Uriah.* ¹⁵ *In it he wrote, "Put Uriah out in front where the fighting is fiercest. Then withdraw from him so he will be struck down and die."* ¹⁶ *So while Joab had the city under siege, he put Uriah at a place where he knew the strongest defenders were.* ¹⁷ *When the men of the city came out and fought against Joab, some of the men in David's army fell; moreover, Uriah the Hittite died.* ¹⁸ *Joab sent David a full account of the battle.* ¹⁹ *He instructed the messenger: "When you have finished giving the king this account of the battle,* ²⁰ *the king's anger may flare up, and he may ask you, 'Why did you get so close to the city to fight? Didn't you know they would shoot arrows from the wall?* ²¹ *Who killed Abimelek son of Jerub-Besheth? Didn't a woman drop an upper millstone on him from the wall, so that he died in Thebez? Why did you get so close to the wall?' If he asks you this, then say to him, 'Moreover, your servant*

Uriah the Hittite is dead.'" ²² *The messenger set out, and when he arrived he told David everything Joab had sent him to say.* ²³ *The messenger said to David, "The men overpowered us and came out against us in the open, but we drove them back to the entrance of the city gate.* ²⁴ *Then the archers shot arrows at your servants from the wall, and some of the king's men died. Moreover, your servant Uriah the Hittite is dead."* ²⁵ *David told the messenger, "Say this to Joab: 'Don't let this upset you; the sword devours one as well as another. Press the attack against the city and destroy it.' Say this to encourage Joab."* ²⁶ *When Uriah's wife heard that her husband was dead, she mourned for him.* ²⁷ *After the time of mourning was over, David had her brought to his house, and she became his wife and bore him a son. But the thing David had done displeased the LORD.*

Notes from group discussion:

_____
_____
_____
_____
_____
_____
_____
_____
_____
_____

Dr. C. White-Elliott

Intelligence
(the ability to apply higher-level thinking)

In education, possessing intelligence is the ability to learn or understand or to deal with new or challenging situations. In psychology, the term may more specifically denote the ability to apply knowledge to manipulate one's environment or to think abstractly as measured by objective criteria (such as the IQ test). Intelligence is usually thought of as deriving from a combination of inherited characteristics and environmental (developmental and social) factors (Encyclopedia Britannica, 2023).

Viewing intelligence through a Christian lens:
From a biblical standpoint, intelligence is the ability to operate within the auspices of God's Word with presence of mind. The Lord gave us free will as part of His unique design for mankind. As intelligent beings, we understand we were created in God's image and are therefore like Him. Therefore, we make the intelligent choice to operate according to His desires instead of as agents of folly.

Use these Bible verses for a better understanding of intelligence. Read each verse. Then, rewrite it in your own words. Doing so will assist in understanding the concept of intelligence better.

II Chronicles 2:12 (NIV)
"And Hiram added: 'Praise be to the LORD, the God of Israel, who made heaven and earth! He has given King David a wise son, endowed with intelligence and discernment, who will build a temple for the LORD and a palace for himself'."

_____
_____
_____

Isaiah 29:14 (NIV)
"Therefore once more I will astound these people with wonder upon wonder; the wisdom of the wise will perish, the intelligence of the intelligent will vanish."

_____

_____

_____

Daniel 5:11 (NIV)
"There is a man in your kingdom who has the spirit of the holy gods in him. In the time of your father he was found to have insight and intelligence and wisdom like that of the gods. Your father, King Nebuchadnezzar, appointed him chief of the magicians, enchanters, astrologers and diviners."

_____

_____

_____

Daniel 5:14 (NIV)
"I have heard that the spirit of the gods is in you and that you have insight, intelligence and outstanding wisdom."

_____

_____

_____

I Corinthians 1:19 (NIV)
"For it is written: 'I will destroy the wisdom of the wise; the intelligence of the intelligent I will frustrate.'"

_____

_____

_____

Proverbs 1:7 (NIV)
"The fear of the Lord is the beginning of knowledge, but fools despise wisdom and instruction."

_____

_____

_____

Proverbs 2:6 (NIV)
"For the Lord gives wisdom; from his mouth come knowledge and understanding."

_____

_____

_____

Personal Reflection

Humans operate in three primary modes: emotionally, ethically, or logically. This also means they may operate in a contrary (negative) position as well. For example, in a given situation, one individual may operate with the emotion of love; whereas, another may operate in the same situation with disdain.

When it comes to being logical, we can be led by our intellect, or we can throw everything we know to be correct out the window. Can you recall a time when you placed logic/intelligence to the side and followed emotion? Write about that time below. Share the outcome of the situation.

What did you learn from the decisions you made?

_____
_____
_____
_____

Would you make the same choice again if the situation were to repeat itself? Why or why not?

_____
_____
_____
_____

What advice would you give to someone regarding using logic/intelligence in everyday life?

_____
_____
_____
_____

Group Discussion
The group discussion for intelligence and wisdom will be combined together under the section on wisdom.

Wisdom

Wisdom is the ability to contemplate and act productively using knowledge, experience, understanding, common sense, and insight (Dictionary, 2023). Wisdom is associated with attributes, such as unbiased judgment, compassion, experiential self-knowledge, self-transcendence, and non-attachment (Grossmann, 2017) and virtues, such as ethics and benevolence (Staudinger & Glück, 2011); (Walsh, 2015).

The Oxford English Dictionary defines wisdom as the "Capacity of judging rightly in matters relating to life and conduct; soundness of judgment in the choice of means and ends; sometimes, less strictly, sound sense, especially in practical affairs: opposed to folly;" also "knowledge (especially of a high or abstruse kind); enlightenment, learning, erudition" (*Oxford English Dictionary*, 2023). Charles Haddon Spurgeon (1871) defined wisdom as "the right use of knowledge."

Viewing wisdom through a Christian lens:

Scripture tells us wisdom is better than gold! These Bible verses about wisdom unlock the keys to gaining insight for your Christian walk. As Christians, we can gain knowledge through the study of God's Word. *"... the wisdom from above is first pure, then peaceable, gentle, open to reason, full of mercy and good fruits, impartial and sincere"* (James 3:17).

Use these Bible verses for a better understanding of wisdom. Read each verse. Then, rewrite it in your own words. Doing so will assist in understanding the concept of wisdom better.

James 3:13 (NIV)
"Who is wise and understanding among you? Let them show it by their good life, by deeds done in the humility that comes from wisdom."

___

___

___

Proverbs 2:6 (NIV)
"For the LORD gives wisdom; from his mouth come knowledge and understanding."

___

___

___

Proverbs 4:7 (NIV)
"The beginning of wisdom is this: Get wisdom. Though it cost all you have, get understanding."

___

___

___

Proverbs 19:8 (NIV)
"The one who gets wisdom loves life; the one who cherishes understanding will soon prosper."

___

___

___

Proverbs 11:2 (NIV)
"When pride comes, then comes disgrace, but with humility comes wisdom."

Proverbs 17:28 (NIV)
"Even fools are thought wise if they keep silent, and discerning if they hold their tongues."

Proverbs 16:16 (NIV)
"How much better to get wisdom than gold, to get insight rather than silver!"

Proverbs 13:10 (NIV)
"Where there is strife, there is pride, but wisdom is found in those who take advice."

___

___

___

Psalm 37:30 (NIV)
"The mouths of the righteous utter wisdom, and their tongues speak what is just."

___

___

___

Ephesians 5:15-16 (NIV)
"Be very careful, then, how you live—not as unwise but as wise, making the most of every opportunity, because the days are evil."

___

___

___

Proverbs 1:7 (NIV)
"The fear of the LORD is the beginning of knowledge, but fools despise wisdom and instruction."

___

___

___

Proverbs 3:7 (NIV)
"Do not be wise in your own eyes; fear the LORD and shun evil."

_____
_____
_____

Proverbs 13:1 (NIV)
"A wise son heeds his father's instruction, but a mocker does not respond to rebukes."

_____
_____
_____

Proverbs 14:1 (NIV)
"The wise woman builds her house, but with her own hands the foolish one tears hers down."

_____
_____
_____

Proverbs 29:11 (NIV)
"Fools give full vent to their rage, but the wise bring calm in the end."

_____
_____
_____

1 Corinthians 1:25 (NIV)
"For the foolishness of God is wiser than human wisdom, and the weakness of God is stronger than human strength."

_____
_____
_____

James 3:17 (NIV)
"But the wisdom that comes from heaven is first of all pure; then peace-loving, considerate, submissive, full of mercy and good fruit, impartial and sincere."

_____
_____
_____

James 1:5 (NIV)
"If any of you lacks wisdom, you should ask God, who gives generously to all without finding fault, and it will be given to you."

_____
_____
_____

Personal Reflection

Describe an instance where you had the wisdom to deal with a situation. Include the details of the situation and the choices that were presented to you.

_____

_____

_____

_____

_____

_____

_____

_____

_____

_____

Which choice did you select and why?

_____

_____

_____

_____

_____

What may have been the outcome if you had selected one of the other options?

_____
_____
_____
_____
_____

Group Discussion (Intelligence and Wisdom)

Intelligence and wisdom are not interchangeable. They are specific characteristics that an individual can embody and behold. However, they do work hand-in-hand. Therefore, the group discussion for intelligence and wisdom is combined in one.

Having knowledge means to have the information; having wisdom means to have insight; having intelligence means to know how to apply the knowledge and/or wisdom.

Proverbs shares the characteristics of the wisdom of ants. Read the following passages and discuss what we as humans can learn from these tiny creatures.

Proverbs 6:6-9 (NIV):

> *Go to the ant, you sluggard; consider its ways and be wise! It has no commander, no overseer or ruler, yet it stores its provisions in summer and gathers its food at harvest.*

Notes from group discussion:

_____
_____

Compassion
(sympathy and empathy)

Compassion is a social feeling that motivates people to go out of their way to relieve the physical, mental, or emotional pains of others and themselves. Compassion is sensitivity to the emotional aspects of the suffering of others. When based on notions such as fairness, justice, and interdependence, it may be considered partially rational in nature.

Compassion involves "feeling for another" and is a precursor to empathy, the "feeling as another" capacity (as opposed to sympathy, the "feeling towards another"). Active compassion is the desire to alleviate another's suffering (Lopez, 2009). Compassion involves allowing ourselves to be moved by suffering to help alleviate and prevent it. An act of compassion is one that is intended to be a helpful act. Other virtues that harmonize with compassion include patience, wisdom, kindness, perseverance, warmth, and resolve.

Viewing compassion through a Christian lens:

The definition of compassion is a feeling of deep sympathy and sorrow for another who is hurting, in pain, or has misfortune and is accompanied by a strong desire to help the suffering. Jesus Christ is the greatest example of someone with true compassion. Not only did Jesus have compassion and heal people from physical suffering, He also showed the greatest compassion for mankind when He died on the cross for our sins.

It is not always easy to show compassion, especially when we feel as though the person deserves his/her misfortune. These Bible verses about compassion teach us that it is a true mark of Christian character. Another great example of someone showing compassion and grace is that of the prodigal son. Read the Scripture below that includes how the father showed compassion on his son (Luke 15:20). Go and do likewise so that you can show the world how Jesus has changed you! (Strong's Commentary, 2023).

Use these Bible verses for a better understanding of compassion. Read each verse. Then, rewrite it in your own words. Doing so will assist in understanding the concept of compassion better.

Exodus 33:19 (NIV)
"And the LORD said, 'I will cause all my goodness to pass in front of you, and I will proclaim my name, the LORD, in your presence. I will have mercy on whom I will have mercy, and I will have compassion on whom I will have compassion'."

_____

_____

_____

II Kings 13:23 (NIV)
"But the LORD was gracious to them and had compassion and showed concern for them because of his covenant with Abraham, Isaac and Jacob. To this day he has been unwilling to destroy them or banish them from his presence."

_____

_____

_____

II Chronicles 30:9 (NIV)
"If you return to the LORD, then your fellow Israelites and your children will be shown compassion by their captors and will return to this land, for the LORD your God is gracious and compassionate. He will not turn his face from you if you return to him."

Nehemiah 9:19 (NIV)
"Because of your great compassion you did not abandon them in the wilderness. By day the pillar of cloud did not fail to guide them on their path, nor the pillar of fire by night to shine on the way they were to take."

Psalm 103:13 (NIV)
"As a father has compassion on his children, so the LORD has compassion on those who fear him."

Psalm 116:5 (NIV)
"The LORD is gracious and righteous; our God is full of compassion."

Daniel 1:9 (NIV)
"Now God had caused the official to show favor and compassion to Daniel."

_____
_____
_____

Isaiah 30:18 (NIV)
"Yet the LORD longs to be gracious to you; therefore he will rise up to show you compassion. For the LORD is a God of justice. Blessed are all who wait for him!"

_____
_____
_____

Jeremiah 42:12 (NIV)
"I will show you compassion so that he will have compassion on you and restore you to your land."

_____
_____
_____

Lamentations 3:32 (NIV)
"Though he brings grief, he will show compassion, so great is his unfailing love."

___

___

___

Zechariah 10:6 (NIV)
"I will strengthen Judah and save the tribes of Joseph. I will restore them because I have compassion on them. They will be as though I had not rejected them, for I am the LORD their God and I will answer them."

___

___

___

Hosea 2:19 (NIV)
"I will betroth you to me forever; I will betroth you in righteousness and justice, in love and compassion."

___

___

___

Malachi 3:17 (NIV)
"'On the day when I act,' says the LORD Almighty, 'they will be my treasured possession. I will spare them, just as a father has compassion and spares his son who serves him'."

___

___

___

Matthew 9:36 (NIV)
"When he saw the crowds, he had compassion on them, because they were harassed and helpless, like sheep without a shepherd."

_____

_____

_____

Luke 15:20 (NIV)
"So he got up and went to his father. 'But while he was still a long way off, his father saw him and was filled with compassion for him; he ran to his son, threw his arms around him and kissed him'."

_____

_____

_____

Romans 9:15 (NIV)
"For he says to Moses, 'I will have mercy on whom I have mercy, and I will have compassion on whom I have compassion'."

_____

_____

_____

II Corinthians 1:3 (NIV)
"Praise be to the God and Father of our Lord Jesus Christ, the Father of compassion and the God of all comfort."

_____

_____

_____

Philippians 2:1 (NIV)
"Therefore if you have any encouragement from being united with Christ, if any comfort from his love, if any common sharing in the Spirit, if any tenderness and compassion."

_____

_____

_____

Colossians 3:12 (NIV)
"Therefore, as God's chosen people, holy and dearly loved, clothe yourselves with compassion, kindness, humility, gentleness and patience."

_____

_____

_____

Personal Reflection

Do you consider yourself a compassionate person? If yes, why? If not, why not?

_____
_____
_____
_____

Provide some examples of when you have shown or lacked compassion.

_____
_____
_____
_____
_____
_____
_____
_____
_____
_____
_____
_____
_____
_____
_____

If you lack compassion, what can you do to become a compassionate person?

___

Do you ever feel at times that you have too much compassion and it can lead you to cause harm to yourself, by being overly kind and compassionate to others? For example, seeing someone in need and giving him/her your grocery money, thereby leaving you without the basic necessities.

___

Group Discussion

When Joseph's older brothers gathered together to form a plot to get rid of him, the majority of them wanted to shed his innocent blood. However, Reuben had compassion upon his younger brother and suggested they not shed his innocent blood. Then, Judah suggested Joseph be sold into slavery instead of being killed. Discuss the positive outcome that eventually resulted from Reuben and Judah's compassion toward Joseph.

Genesis 37:18-36 (NIV)

> *But they saw him in the distance, and before he reached them, they plotted to kill him. [19] "Here comes that dreamer!" they said to each other. [20] "Come now, let's kill him and throw him into one of these cisterns and say that a ferocious animal devoured him. Then we'll see what comes of his dreams." [21] When Reuben heard this, he tried to rescue him from their hands. "Let's not take his life," he said. [22] "Don't shed any blood. Throw him into this cistern here in the wilderness, but don't lay a hand on him." Reuben said this to rescue him from them and take him back to his father. [23] So when Joseph came to his brothers, they stripped him of his robe—the ornate robe he was wearing— [24] and they took him and threw him into the cistern. The cistern was empty; there was no water in it. [25] As they sat down to eat their meal, they looked up and saw a caravan of Ishmaelites coming from Gilead. Their camels were loaded with spices, balm and myrrh, and they were on their way to take them down to Egypt. [26] Judah said to his brothers, "What will we gain if we kill our brother and cover up his blood? [27] Come, let's sell him to the Ishmaelites and not lay our hands on him; after all, he is our brother, our own flesh and blood." His brothers agreed. [28] So when the Midianite merchants came by, his brothers pulled Joseph up out of the cistern and sold him for twenty shekels of silver to the Ishmaelites, who took him to Egypt. [29] When Reuben returned to the cistern and saw that Joseph was not there, he tore*

his clothes. ³⁰ He went back to his brothers and said, "The boy isn't there! Where can I turn now?" ³¹ Then they got Joseph's robe, slaughtered a goat and dipped the robe in the blood. ³² They took the ornate robe back to their father and said, "We found this. Examine it to see whether it is your son's robe." ³³ He recognized it and said, "It is my son's robe! Some ferocious animal has devoured him. Joseph has surely been torn to pieces." ³⁴ Then Jacob tore his clothes, put on sackcloth and mourned for his son many days. ³⁵ All his sons and daughters came to comfort him, but he refused to be comforted. "No," he said, "I will continue to mourn until I join my son in the grave." So his father wept for him. ³⁶ Meanwhile, the Midianites sold Joseph in Egypt to Potiphar, one of Pharaoh's officials, the captain of the guard.

Notes from group discussion:

_____
_____
_____
_____
_____
_____
_____
_____
_____
_____

Humility

Humility is the quality of being humble (Wiktionary, 2023). Dictionary definitions accentuate humility as low self-regard and sense of unworthiness (Snyder & Lopez, 2001). Humility is an outward expression of an appropriate inner, or self-regard, and is contrasted with humiliation, which is an imposition, often external, of shame upon a person. Humility may be misappropriated as ability to suffer humiliation through self-denouncements, which remains focused on self rather than being low in self-focus (Schwarzer, 2012; Greenberg, Koole & Pyszczynski, 2013).

Viewing humility through a Christian lens:
We know from God's Word that He resists the proud and gives grace to the humble. How can we know we are living in humility and ready to receive God's blessings? Humility is the ability to be without pride or arrogance, and it is a principal character that should be seen in those who follow Jesus Christ. Jesus is the best example of someone who humbly followed God's plan for His life.

Proverbs is filled with warnings of those who refuse to be humble. The New Testament is full of blessings for those who put others before themselves. You will miss out on the blessed, abundant life God wants for you if you refuse to let go of pride and follow His purpose in your life. Be encouraged by these Bible verses about humility and start choosing today to come humbly before God, so He can lift you up! (Strong's Commentary, 2023).

Use these Bible verses for a better understanding of humility. Read each verse. Then, rewrite it in your own words. Doing so will assist in understanding the concept of humility better.

Psalm 45:4 (NIV)
"In your majesty ride forth victoriously in the cause of truth, humility and justice; let your right hand achieve awesome deeds."

_____
_____
_____

Proverbs 11:2 (NIV)
"When pride comes, then comes disgrace, but with humility comes wisdom.

_____
_____
_____

Proverbs 15:33 (NIV)
"Wisdom's instruction is to fear the LORD, and humility comes before honor."

_____
_____
_____

Proverbs 18:12 (NIV)
"Before a downfall the heart is haughty, but humility comes before honor."

_____
_____
_____

Proverbs 22:4 (NIV)

"Humility is the fear of the LORD; its wages are riches and honor and life."

_____

_____

_____

Zephaniah 2:3 (NIV)

"Seek the LORD, all you humble of the land, you who do what he commands. Seek righteousness, seek humility; perhaps you will be sheltered on the day of the LORD's anger."

_____

_____

_____

Acts 20:19 (NIV)

"I served the Lord with great humility and with tears and in the midst of severe testing by the plots of my Jewish opponents."

_____

_____

_____

II Corinthians 10:1 (NIV)

"By the humility and gentleness of Christ, I appeal to you—I, Paul, who am 'timid' when face to face with you, but 'bold' toward you when away!"

Philippians 2:3 (NIV)
"Do nothing out of selfish ambition or vain conceit. Rather, in humility value others above yourselves."

Colossians 2:18 (NIV)
"Do not let anyone who delights in false humility and the worship of angels disqualify you. Such a person also goes into great detail about what they have seen; they are puffed up with idle notions by their unspiritual mind."

Colossians 2:23 (NIV)
"Such regulations indeed have an appearance of wisdom, with their self-imposed worship, their false humility and their harsh treatment of the body, but they lack any value in restraining sensual indulgence."

Colossians 3:12 (NIV)
"Therefore, as God's chosen people, holy and dearly loved, clothe yourselves with compassion, kindness, humility, gentleness and patience."

_____
_____
_____

James 3:13 (NIV)
"Who is wise and understanding among you? Let them show it by their good life, by deeds done in the humility that comes from wisdom."

_____
_____
_____

I Peter 5:5 (NIV)
"In the same way, you who are younger, submit yourselves to your elders. All of you, clothe yourselves with humility toward one another, because, 'God opposes the proud but shows favor to the humble'."

_____
_____
_____

Personal Reflection

Do you embody the spirit of humility? How do you know whether you are humble or not? Answer by providing examples of your behavior, thoughts, or words that demonstrate humility or a lack thereof.

_____
_____
_____
_____
_____
_____
_____
_____
_____
_____

If you are not walking in the spirit of humility, what can you do to change your thinking, behavior, and words to those than would be acceptable in the sight of the Lord?

_____
_____
_____
_____

Living Life **WITHOUT A MASK** Authentically & Unapologetically You!

_____
_____
_____
_____
_____
_____
_____

Group Discussion

Read the following account of young Moses and his interaction with the Egyptians. How did Moses put the needs of his fellow Hebrews before his own needs, according to the following excerpt?

Exodus 2:11-12 (NIV)

> *One day, after Moses had grown up, he went out to where his own people were and watched them at their hard labor. He saw an Egyptian beating a Hebrew, one of his own people.* [12] *Looking this way and that and seeing no one, he killed the Egyptian and hid him in the sand.*

Notes from group discussion:

_____
_____
_____
_____
_____

Patience
(endurance/forbearance)

Patience (or forbearance) is the ability to endure difficult circumstances. Patience may involve perseverance in the face of delay; tolerance of provocation without responding with disrespect or anger; forbearance when under strain, especially when faced with longer-term difficulties; or being able to wait for a long time without getting irritated or bored. Patience is also used to refer to the character trait of being steadfast.

Viewing patience through a Christian lens:
Patience is a virtue that is often discussed in the Bible. In fact, patience is one of the fruits of the Holy Spirit listed in Galatians 5:22-23. The Bible teaches patience is an important aspect of our relationship with God and our relationships with others. One of the most well-known verses about patience is found in James 1:3-4, which says, *"For you know that when your faith is tested, your endurance has a chance to grow. So let it grow, for when your endurance is fully developed, you will be perfect and complete, needing nothing."*

The Bible also teaches us to be patient in our interactions with others. In Colossians 3:12-13, we are encouraged to *"clothe ourselves with compassion, kindness, humility, gentleness and patience"* when dealing with others. We are reminded to be patient with those who may be difficult or challenging to love. Ultimately, the Bible teaches us patience is an important aspect of our spiritual growth and our relationships with others. By cultivating patience, we can become more like Christ and better reflect His love to the world around us.

Use these Bible verses for a better understanding of patience. Read each verse. Then, rewrite it in your own words. Doing so will assist in understanding the concept of patience better.

Romans 12:12 (NIV)
"Rejoice in hope, be patient in tribulation, be constant in prayer."

_____
_____
_____

Galatians 6:9 (NIV)
"And let us not grow weary of doing good, for in due season we will reap, if we do not give up."

_____
_____
_____

Romans 8:25 (NIV)
"But if we hope for what we do not see, we wait for it with patience."

_____
_____
_____

Ephesians 4:2 (NIV)
"With all humility and gentleness, with patience, bearing with one another in love."

_____
_____
_____

Psalm 37:7-9 (NIV)
"Be still before the Lord and wait patiently for him; fret not yourself over the one who prospers in his way, over the man who carries out evil devices! Refrain from anger, and forsake wrath! Fret not yourself; it tends only to evil. For the evildoers shall be cut off, but those who wait for the Lord shall inherit the land."

Proverbs 19:11 (NIV)
"A person's wisdom yields patience; it is to one's glory to overlook an offense."

Proverbs 25:15 (NIV)
"Through patience a ruler can be persuaded, and a gentle tongue can break a bone."

Ecclesiastes 7:8 (NIV)
"The end of a matter is better than its beginning, and patience is better than pride."

Isaiah 7:13 (NIV)

"Then Isaiah said, 'Hear now, you house of David! Is it not enough to try the patience of humans? Will you try the patience of my God also?'"

Romans 2:4 (NIV)

"Or do you show contempt for the riches of his kindness, forbearance and patience, not realizing that God's kindness is intended to lead you to repentance?"

Romans 9:22 (NIV)

"What if God, although choosing to show his wrath and make his power known, bore with great patience the objects of his wrath—prepared for destruction?"

II Corinthians 6:6 (NIV)
"in purity, understanding, patience and kindness; in the Holy Spirit and in sincere love"

_____
_____
_____

Colossians 1:11 (NIV)
"being strengthened with all power according to his glorious might so that you may have great endurance and patience"

_____
_____
_____

Colossians 3:12 (NIV)
"Therefore, as God's chosen people, holy and dearly loved, clothe yourselves with compassion, kindness, humility, gentleness and patience."

_____
_____
_____

I Timothy 1:16 (NIV)
"But for that very reason I was shown mercy so that in me, the worst of sinners, Christ Jesus might display his immense patience as an example for those who would believe in him and receive eternal life."

II Timothy 3:10 (NIV)
"You, however, know all about my teaching, my way of life, my purpose, faith, patience, love, endurance."

II Timothy 4:2 (NIV)
"Preach the word; be prepared in season and out of season; correct, rebuke and encourage—with great patience and careful instruction."

Hebrews 6:12 (NIV)
"We do not want you to become lazy, but to imitate those who through faith and patience inherit what has been promised."

James 5:10 (NIV)
"Brothers and sisters, as an example of patience in the face of suffering, take the prophets who spoke in the name of the Lord."

_____

_____

_____

II Peter 3:15 (NIV)
"Bear in mind that our Lord's patience means salvation, just as our dear brother Paul also wrote you with the wisdom that God gave him."

_____

_____

_____

Personal Reflection

Do you consider yourself to be a patient person? Why or why not?

_____
_____

Provide examples to demonstrate your level of patience in three different situations (choose from your personal life, in the workplace, with family, at church, etc). Try to choose instances from different time frames of your life (teenage years, young adult, as a parent, as a mature adult) to demonstrate your development.

Situation 1:

_____
_____
_____
_____
_____
_____

Situation 2:

_____
_____
_____
_____
_____

Situation 3:

What did you learn about your level of patience after recalling those three situations?

Group Discussion
Read the following excerpted account of Job's trials and the patience he demonstrated throughout it all.

According to the Bible, Job was a devout man who always prayed and worshipped God. Furthermore, he was known as a patient man (James 5:11). God spoke highly of His servant Job and his faithfulness to Him (Job 1:1, 8). God brought Satan's attention to Job's love for God, which made Satan jealous. Satan issued a challenge to God, and God accepted it with a condition.

Here is the conversation between God and Satan concerning Job.

God: *"Have you considered my servant Job, that there is none like him on the earth, a blameless and upright man who fears God and turns away from evil?"* (Job 1:8 ESV).

Satan: *"Does Job fear God for no reason? Have you not put a hedge around him and his house and all that he has, on every side? You have blessed the work of his hands, and his possessions have increased in the land. But stretch out your hand and touch all that he has, and he will curse you to your face"* (Job 1:9-11 ESV).

God: *"Behold, all that he has is in your hand. Only against him do not stretch out your hand"* (Job 1:12 ESV).

So, Satan began to remove all Job had, hoping Job would curse God to His face.

One day while at home, one of Job's servants came to him and reported that the Sabeans had stolen all of Job's oxen and donkeys and killed the attending servants (Job 1:13-15). Before Job could digest the news, another servant came and told him fire from heaven had destroyed all his sheep and the servants looking after the sheep (Job 1:16). Yet again, while Job was hearing the bad news of the second messenger, another servant joined in. The third servant told Job the Chaldeans had stolen his entire stock of mules and killed the workers (Job 1:17).

All the bad news was enough to make Job start worrying. However, the news about Job's property being stolen was nothing compared to the fourth and last servant who arrived. Before Job could process the news about the thefts and the deaths, the final blow was yet to come. A final servant came to Job and told him a desert wind had knocked down the house where all his sons and daughters were having a party (Job 1:18).

This last news would have havoc on any sane man's mind. Yet, Job kept his head. Instead of blaming God, Job fell on His face in worship and reverence to the Almighty Lord (Job 1:20-22).

Satan was not satisfied stopping there; instead, he continued his evil test on Job by bringing sickness to him through painful boils appearing on his skin (Job 2:7).

However, the Bible says in everything that Satan tried to defeat Job; Job did not sin or blame God for all the bad things that happened to him (Job 2:10).

God told Job about his suffering by giving two answers. First, the Lord reminded Job that He (God) was in charge of the universe and that He had not fallen asleep (Job 38-39). God's first response made Job understand that the great universe in which he lived could only function due to God's mighty power that keeps everything in place. God's first point, therefore, is letting Job know He has everything under control. Nothing can fall out of place unless He allows it, even humanity's suffering. Job responded to God by saying, *"Behold, I am insignificant; what can I reply to you? I lay my hand on my mouth. Once I have spoken, and I will not answer; even twice, and I will add nothing more"* (Job 40:3-5 NASB 1995).

God's second point was to ask whether Job had the power to control the creatures He had made, like the Leviathan, a dangerous creature that lives far away from human interference (Job 40-41). Of course, Job's answer was a resounding no. God's point is this: if Job cannot control such a dangerous creature, how can he control the events in his life? Only God has total control over the events in every human being's life. In both points, God helped Job see that He controls everything that happens, regardless of how bad the situation seems.

In your group discussion, explore all Job suffered and experienced and how his love, respect, and adoration for the Lord remained intact. Yes, there were times of frustration, but through Job's patient love for God, he never turned his back on the Lord or cursed His name.

Notes from group discussion:

_____

_____

_____

_____

_____

_____

_____

_____

_____

_____

_____

_____

_____

_____

_____

_____

Dedication
(commitment)

According to the Oxford Dictionary (2023), dedication is "The giving up or devoting (of oneself, one's time, labour, etc.) to the service of a person or to the pursuit of a purpose."

Viewing dedication through a Christian lens:
From a spiritual perspective, to be dedicated is to give of one's self for the service of God within His Kingdom. In biblical days, people dedicated themselves and objects for God's service. Also, specific items can be used in dedication services, such as oil, which represents God's anointing.

Use these Bible verses for a better understanding of dedication. Read each verse. Then, rewrite it in your own words. Doing so will assist in understanding the concept of dedication better.

Leviticus 21:12 (NIV)
"...nor leave the sanctuary of his God or desecrate it, because he has been dedicated by the anointing oil of his God. I am the LORD."

_____
_____
_____

Leviticus 27:8 (NIV)
"If anyone making the vow is too poor to pay the specified amount, the person being dedicated is to be presented to the priest, who will set the value according to what the one making the vow can afford."

_____

_____

_____

Numbers 18:6 (NIV)
"I myself have selected your fellow Levites from among the Israelites as a gift to you, dedicated to the LORD to do the work at the tent of meeting."

_____

_____

_____

Judges 13:5 (NIV)
"You will become pregnant and have a son whose head is never to be touched by a razor because the boy is to be a Nazirite, dedicated to God from the womb. He will take the lead in delivering Israel from the hands of the Philistines."

_____

_____

_____

II Samuel 8:11 (NIV)
"King David dedicated these articles to the LORD, as he had done with the silver and gold from all the nations he had subdued."

_____

_____

_____

II Samuel 8:12 (NIV)
"Edom and Moab, the Ammonites and the Philistines, and Amalek. He also dedicated the plunder taken from Hadadezer son of Rehob, king of Zobah."

_____

_____

_____

I Kings 7:51 (NIV)
"When all the work King Solomon had done for the temple of the LORD was finished, he brought in the things his father David had dedicated—the silver and gold and the furnishings—and he placed them in the treasuries of the LORD's temple."

_____

_____

_____

I Kings 8:63 (NIV)
"Solomon offered a sacrifice of fellowship offerings to the LORD: twenty-two thousand cattle and a hundred and twenty thousand sheep and goats. So the king and all the Israelites dedicated the temple of the LORD."

_____

_____

_____

I Kings 15:15 (NIV)
"He brought into the temple of the LORD the silver and gold and the articles that he and his father had dedicated."

_____
_____
_____

I Chronicles 26:20 (NIV)
"Their fellow Levites were in charge of the treasuries of the house of God and the treasuries for the dedicated things."

_____
_____
_____

I Chronicles 26:27 (NIV)
"Some of the plunder taken in battle they dedicated for the repair of the temple of the LORD."

_____
_____
_____

Personal Reflection

What you have you dedicated yourself to over the last few years? Have you honored your commitment? If so, how? If not, how and why did you break the commitment you made?

_____
_____
_____
_____
_____
_____
_____
_____

If there is a commitment that you did not honor as you had originally intended, what can you do to get back on track?

_____
_____
_____
_____
_____
_____
_____
_____

Group Discussion

In the following passages (Luke 22:31-34, 54-62, NIV), read the account of Simon Peter, one of Jesus' twelve disciples, who had dedicated himself to the service of the Lord.

Did Peter remain dedicated? Why or why not? What changed for Peter?

> *Jesus said, [31] "Simon, Simon, Satan has asked to sift all of you as wheat. [32] But I have prayed for you, Simon, that your faith may not fail. And when you have turned back, strengthen your brothers." [33] But he replied, "Lord, I am ready to go with you to prison and to death." [34] Jesus answered, "I tell you, Peter, before the rooster crows today, you will deny three times that you know me."*
>
> *[54] Then seizing him (Jesus), they led him away and took him into the house of the high priest. Peter followed at a distance. [55] And when some there had kindled a fire in the middle of the courtyard and had sat down together, Peter sat down with them. [56] A servant girl saw him seated there in the firelight. She looked closely at him and said, "This man was with him." [57] But he denied it. "Woman, I don't know him," he said. [58] A little later someone else saw him and said, "You also are one of them." "Man, I am not!" Peter replied. [59] About an hour later another asserted, "Certainly this fellow was with him, for he is a Galilean." [60] Peter replied, "Man, I don't know what you're talking about!" Just as he was speaking, the rooster crowed. [61] The Lord turned and looked straight at Peter. Then Peter remembered the word the Lord had spoken to him: "Before the rooster crows today, you will disown me three times." [62] And he went outside and wept bitterly.*

Notes from group discussion:

_____

_____

Living Life **WITHOUT A MASK** Authentically & Unapologetically You!

Discipline
(focus)

Discipline is training that produces obedience or self-control, often in the form of rules and punishments if these are broken, or the obedience of self-control produced by this training. It is also the ability to train one's focus on a particular task or lifestyle.

Viewing discipline through a Christian lens:
God's Word tells us that all discipline is necessary for training toward righteousness. No one likes to be disciplined or to give discipline, but when it is godly discipline, it comes from a place of love. Love is what drives parents to teach their children the right way of living. Throughout Scripture, God the Father, teaches and leads us, His children, away from sin and toward holiness through discipline.

Use these Bible verses for a better understanding of discipline. Read each verse. Then, rewrite it in your own words. Doing so will assist in understanding the concept of discipline better.

Deuteronomy 4:36 (NIV)
"From heaven he made you hear his voice to discipline you. On earth he showed you his great fire, and you heard his words from out of the fire."

_____
_____
_____

Job 5:17 (NIV)
"Blessed is the one whom God corrects; so do not despise the discipline of the Almighty."

Psalm 94:12 (NIV)
"Blessed is the one you discipline, LORD, the one you teach from your law."

Proverbs 3:11 (NIV)
"My son, do not despise the LORD's discipline, and do not resent his rebuke."

Proverbs 5:23 (NIV)
"For lack of discipline they will die, led astray by their own great folly."

Proverbs 10:17 (NIV)
"Whoever heeds discipline shows the way to life, but whoever ignores correction leads others astray."

Proverbs 13:18 (NIV)
"Whoever disregards discipline comes to poverty and shame, but whoever heeds correction is honored."

Proverbs 13:24 (NIV)
"Whoever spares the rod hates their children, but the one who loves their children is careful to discipline them."

Proverbs 15:5 (NIV)
"A fool spurns a parent's discipline, but whoever heeds correction shows prudence."

___

___

___

Proverbs 19:20 (NIV)
"Listen to advice and accept discipline, and at the end you will be counted among the wise."

___

___

___

Proverbs 22:15 (NIV)
"Folly is bound up in the heart of a child, but the rod of discipline will drive it far away."

___

___

___

I Corinthians 4:21 (NIV)
"What do you prefer? Shall I come to you with a rod of discipline, or shall I come in love and with a gentle spirit?"

___

___

___

Hebrews 12:7 (NIV)
"Endure hardship as discipline; God is treating you as his children. For what children are not disciplined by their father?"

_____
_____
_____

Hebrews 12:11 (NIV)
"No discipline seems pleasant at the time, but painful. Later on, however, it produces a harvest of righteousness and peace for those who have been trained by it."

_____
_____
_____

Revelation 3:19 (NIV)
"Those whom I love I rebuke and discipline. So be earnest and repent."

_____
_____
_____

Personal Reflection

How do you exercise discipline in your life as it relates to God's Word?

_____

_____

_____

_____

_____

_____

_____

What do you do when you find yourself tempted to stray from the disciplinary measures you have placed in your life?

_____

_____

_____

_____

_____

_____

_____

_____

Group Discussion

Read about the Prodigal Son in Luke 15:11-31 (NIV). Discuss how the son was not content to wait to receive his inheritance at the appointed time and the trouble he landed in.

Jesus continued: "There was a man who had two sons. ¹² The younger one said to his father, 'Father, give me my share of the estate.' So he divided his property between them. ¹³ "Not long after that, the younger son got together all he had, set off for a distant country and there squandered his wealth in wild living. ¹⁴ After he had spent everything, there was a severe famine in that whole country, and he began to be in need. ¹⁵ So he went and hired himself out to a citizen of that country, who sent him to his fields to feed pigs. ¹⁶ He longed to fill his stomach with the pods that the pigs were eating, but no one gave him anything. ¹⁷ "When he came to his senses, he said, 'How many of my father's hired servants have food to spare, and here I am starving to death! ¹⁸ I will set out and go back to my father and say to him: Father, I have sinned against heaven and against you. ¹⁹ I am no longer worthy to be called your son; make me like one of your hired servants.' ²⁰ So he got up and went to his father. "But while he was still a long way off, his father saw him and was filled with compassion for him; he ran to his son, threw his arms around him and kissed him. ²¹ "The son said to him, 'Father, I have sinned against heaven and against you. I am no longer worthy to be called your son.' ²² "But the father said to his servants, 'Quick! Bring the best robe and put it on him. Put a ring on his finger and sandals on his feet. ²³ Bring the fattened calf and kill it. Let's have a feast and celebrate. ²⁴ For this son of mine was dead and is alive again; he was lost and is found.' So they began to celebrate. ²⁵ "Meanwhile, the older son was in the field. When he came near the house, he heard music and dancing. ²⁶ So he called one of the servants and asked him what was going on. ²⁷ 'Your brother has come,' he replied, 'and your father has killed the *fattened calf because he has him back safe and sound.'* [28] *"The older brother became angry and refused to go in. So his father went out and pleaded with him.* [29] *But he answered his father, 'Look! All these years I've been slaving for you and never disobeyed your orders. Yet you never gave me even a young goat so I could celebrate with my friends.* [30] *But when this son of yours who has squandered your property with prostitutes comes home, you kill the fattened calf for him!'* [31] *"'My son,' the father said, 'you are always with me, and everything I have is yours.* [32] *But we had to celebrate and be glad, because this brother of yours was dead and is alive again; he was lost and is found.'"*

Notes from group discussion:

_____
_____
_____
_____
_____
_____
_____
_____
_____
_____
_____
_____

Dr. C. White-Elliott

Contentment
(personal satisfaction)

Contentment is a state of being where one is satisfied with his/her current situation, and the state of affairs in one's life as they presently are. If one is content, he/she is pleased with his/her situation and how the elements in one's life are situated. Contrary to popular belief, it is possible to be content with one's life regardless of the circumstance, regardless of whether things are going as one expected or not ("Contentment: What it is and Why it Matters," 2020).

Viewing contentment through a Christian lens:
According to the Bible, contentment is a state of being satisfied, at peace, and emotionally fulfilled with what one has or the circumstances in which one finds him/herself. It is an attitude of the heart and mind that is not dependent on external possessions, wealth, or circumstances. Bible verses about contentment teaches us that it comes from recognizing and being satisfied with God's provision in one's life, whether that provision is material, relational, or spiritual. It involves trusting that God knows what is best and provides for our needs.

Scripture helps us understand true contentment includes the ability to accept and find peace in one's current circumstances, even if they are challenging. Apostle Paul, in Philippians 4:11-12, speaks of learning to be content in any situation. Contentment is linked to trusting in God's sovereignty and His plan for one's life. It acknowledges that God is in control and has a purpose for everything, even in difficult times. As we trust God, give thanks in all circumstances, and find freedom from worry and anxiety, we will experience God's presence and peace! Bible verses on contentment will help you become rooted in God's Word and gain a faith perspective filled with an inner and outer attitude of being blessed by God's provision.

Use these Bible verses for a better understanding of contentment. Read each verse. Then, rewrite it in your own words. Doing so will assist in understanding the concept of contentment better.

Genesis 25:27 (NIV)
"The boys grew up, and Esau became a skillful hunter, a man of the open country, while Jacob was content to stay at home among the tents."

_____
_____
_____

Joshua 7:7 (NIV)
"And Joshua said, 'Alas, Sovereign LORD, why did you ever bring this people across the Jordan to deliver us into the hands of the Amorites to destroy us? If only we had been content to stay on the other side of the Jordan!'"

_____
_____
_____

Psalm 131:2 (NIV)
"But I have calmed and quieted myself, I am like a weaned child with its mother; like a weaned child I am content."

_____
_____
_____

Proverbs 13:25 (NIV)
"The righteous eat to their hearts' content, but the stomach of the wicked goes hungry."

_____
_____
_____

Proverbs 19:23 (NIV)
"The fear of the LORD leads to life; then one rests content, untouched by trouble."

_____
_____
_____

Ecclesiastes 4:8 (NIV)
"There was a man all alone; he had neither son nor brother. There was no end to his toil, yet his eyes were not content with his wealth. 'For whom am I toiling,' he asked, 'and why am I depriving myself of enjoyment?" This too is meaningless— a miserable business!'"

_____
_____
_____

Luke 3:14 (NIV)
Then some soldiers asked him, 'And what should we do?' He replied, 'Don't extort money and don't accuse people falsely—be content with your pay'."

Philippians 4:11-12 (NIV)
"I am not saying this because I am in need, for I have learned to be content whatever the circumstances. I know what it is to be in need, and I know what it is to have plenty. I have learned the secret of being content in any and every situation, whether well fed or hungry, whether living in plenty or in want."

I Timothy 6:8 (NIV)
"But if we have food and clothing, we will be content with that."

Hebrews 13:5 (NIV)
"Keep your lives free from the love of money and be content with what you have."

Job 36:11 (NIV)
"If they obey and serve him, they will spend the rest of their days in prosperity and their years in contentment."

_____
_____
_____

I Timothy 6:6 (NIV)
"But godliness with contentment is great gain."

_____
_____
_____

Personal Reflection

Are you content with the present circumstances in your life (career, education, relationships, finances, spiritual walk)? Why or why not?

_____
_____
_____
_____
_____
_____
_____
_____

Does being content include not aspiring to greater heights? Explain your answer.

_____
_____
_____
_____
_____
_____
_____
_____

Group Discussion

Read the Parable of the Lost Sheep in Luke 15:3-7 (NIV). Explain why it was okay for the shepherd to lack contentment when one of the sheep was lost.

> *Then Jesus told them this parable: "Suppose one of you has a hundred sheep and loses one of them. Doesn't he leave the ninety-nine in the open country and go after the lost sheep until he finds it? And when he finds it, he joyfully puts it on his shoulders and goes home. Then he calls his friends and neighbors together and says, 'Rejoice with me; I have found my lost sheep.' I tell you that in the same way there will be more rejoicing in heaven over one sinner who repents than over ninety-nine righteous persons who do not need to repent."*

Notes from group discussion:

_____
_____
_____
_____
_____
_____
_____
_____
_____
_____
_____

Many of you may be familiar with the fruit of the Spirit: love, joy, peace, forbearance, kindness, goodness, faithfulness, gentleness, and self-control. When we first come to Christ, we may not embody any or all of the nine fruit. However, they can all be developed and attained over time. Gaining the fruit of the Spirit is the direct result of walking with God. As we grow in our relationship with God, our fight against sin and our love for God and others grows stronger and leads us to grow in love, joy, peace, patience, kindness, goodness, faithfulness, gentleness, and self-control.

In the same way, if we lack the characteristics of integrity, intelligence, wisdom, compassion, humility, patience, dedication, discipline, and contentment, they can be added to us as we cling to the Lord and His Word. Both the fruit of the Spirit and the aforementioned characteristics are added purposefully as we focus on self-improvement.

Chapter Two
Why the Mask?

Chapter Two
Why the Mask?

Now that you have gone through the task of discovering the characteristics that comprise your personal makeup and understand which you are lacking, it is time to understand whether or not you wear a mask and why.

The two primary reasons people wear masks are
1. to hide their true identity for the purpose of escaping judgment, and
2. to shield their insecurities.

Avoiding Scrutiny and Judgment

Our world system is filled with judgment. Everything that is said, done, and attempted is discussed at length and scrutinized. And, people, regardless of nationality, race, creed, color, sexual orientation, or religious affiliation, are judged, resulting in either praise or negative criticism. We are judged regarding every manner of our lives from our personality, our career choice, our education level, our income bracket, the geographical location of our home, how we raise our children, our eating/dietary habits, our choice of attire, how spiritual we are or are not, who our friends are, the vehicle we drive, our credit worthiness, our weight, and the list goes on. And who judges us? Our friends, our family, our coworkers, our mate, the media, church members, neighbors, creditors, etc. When are we judged? Every day, all day, from the time the sun rises to well after it has set. Where are we judged? On social media, via text messages, during phone calls, in sermons, face to face, and inadvertently (which ironically may be the most common method because some people lack directness).

Being judged is one of the harsh realities of life, and it can be hurtful and damaging. Consequently, people go to self-defeating lengths to elude the possibility of being negatively judged by others. They avoid telling people what they want to tell them. They don't speak up in class or during work meetings. They avoid telling their mate their true desires. They don't ask for a raise. They won't tell a new date where they would like to go for dinner. They cover up their perceived imperfections and failures.

This fear of judgment is linked to the desire to be liked by all at all times. Which, of course, is impossible. And because that is impossible, it is a losing game that keeps people from experiencing and expressing their true self. Instead, they desire to be the self who everyone enjoys, praises, smiles at, and ego strokes.

Let's face it- people are always judging others - good/bad or like/dislike, with use of words and symbols 👍 👎 ♥. One positive response can make someone's day, while one negative response can ruin someone's life. That is how much weight is placed on the words and actions of other people, even strangers.

Shielding Insecurities

The second reason people wear masks is to shield their insecurities from onlookers. We are all insecure about something, but it is how we deal with our insecurities that will determine our outcome in life and whether we will experience true joy or not on a daily basis rather than the temporal emotion happiness, which is fleeting and predicated upon outside circumstances.

Insecurity is a common feeling people will experience at some point, and it can stem from numerous sources. Generally, it presents as a lack of confidence, anxiety, and uncertainty.

Insecurity involves an overall sense of uncertainty or anxiety about your worth, abilities, skills, and value as a person, which is sometimes a result of comparing yourself to others. The negative impacts of insecurity could be physical, mental, or emotional. Without security, you cannot accomplish full trust or function to your fullest potential. Life experiences can also affect a person's level of insecurity.

Possible causes of insecurity include:
1. Lack of family emotional support: People with a loving, supportive family are less likely to deal with insecurity.
2. Lack of physiological needs/satisfaction: When people are insecure in their food, housing, and safety needs, they struggle to move on to satisfying psychological needs like security.
3. Lack of emotional intelligence: Those with low emotional intelligence cannot accurately monitor the feelings of themselves and others, leading to unhealthy relationships and less trust.
4. Lack of openness: When people aren't open, curious, and comfortable with new people and situations, they note more stress and fear, resulting in lower security.
5. Lack of agreeableness: Disagreeable people tend to have more interpersonal conflicts due to not being helpful, supportive, or empathetic. These qualities produce a sense of risk in social situations and less security.
6. An underlying mental health condition: Mental health conditions like anxiety and depression have a bidirectional relationship with insecurity. Personality disorders like borderline personality disorder and narcissistic personality disorder also have a connection to insecurity.
7. An over-dependence on others: As people become dependent on people or relationships, their insecurity grows as they perceive risk in the relationship ending.

Insecurity can originate from several sources and branch out into multiple areas of one's life. Because it has different origins and effects, one person's insecurity can look completely different from another's. Not all forms fit neatly into categories either, but some of the most common types of insecurity include relationship insecurity, social insecurity, body image insecurity, job insecurity, and insecurity of basic needs (Patterson, 2022). And because people do not tend to wear their insecurities on their sleeves, they wear masks to cover them as to not expose themselves to negative responses or ridicule from others.

Continue reading and continue to perform a self-assessment upon the characteristics you embody. In the last chapter, we surveyed positive endearing characteristics. Now, let us examine characteristics that possibly lead to covering up. Remember, be honest with yourself, so you can be the best you that you could ever be.

Shame & Embarrassment

Shame is a discrete, basic emotion, described as a moral or social emotion that drives people to hide or deny their wrongdoings (Tracy & Robins, 2007; Shein, 2018). Moral emotions are emotions that have an influence on a person's decision-making skills and monitors different social behaviors (Shein, 2018). The focus of shame is on the self or the individual with respect to a perceived audience. It can bring about profound feelings of deficiency, defeat, inferiority, unworthiness, or self-loathing. Our attention turns inward; we isolate from our surroundings and withdraw into closed-off self-absorption. Not only do we feel alienated from others but also from the healthy parts of ourselves. The alienation from the world is replaced with painful emotions and self-deprecating thoughts and inner anguish (Lancer, 2014). Shame can also be described as an unpleasant self-conscious emotion that involves negative evaluation of one's self (Parsa, 2018). Shame can be a painful emotion that is seen as a "...comparison of the self's action with the self's standards..." but may equally stem from comparison of the self's state of being with the ideal social context's standard.

Embarrassment is an emotional state that is associated with mild to severe levels of discomfort, and which is usually experienced when someone commits (or thinks of) a socially unacceptable or frowned-upon act that is witnessed by or revealed to others. Frequently grouped with shame and guilt, embarrassment is considered a "self-conscious emotion," and it can have a profoundly negative impact on a person's thoughts or behavior ("Embarrassment," *Psychology Today*). Usually, some perception of loss of honor or dignity (or other high-value ideals) is involved, but the embarrassment level and the type depend on the situation.

Viewing shame through a Christian lens:

Shame is a consequence of sin. Feelings of guilt and shame are subjective acknowledgments of an objective spiritual reality. Guilt is judicial in character; shame is relational. Though related to guilt, shame emphasizes sin's effect on self-identity. Sinful human beings are traumatized before a holy God, exposed for failure to live up to God's glorious moral purpose.

Use these Bible verses for a better understanding of shame. Read each verse. Then, rewrite it in your own words. Doing so will assist in understanding the concept of shame better.

Romans 10:11 (NIV)
"As Scripture says, 'Anyone who believes in him will never be put to shame'."

_____

_____

_____

I Corinthians 15:34 (NIV)
"Come back to your senses as you ought, and stop sinning; for there are some who are ignorant of God—I say this to your shame."

_____

_____

_____

Psalm 31:1 (NIV)
"In you, Lord, I have taken refuge; let me never be put to shame; deliver me in your righteousness."

_____
_____
_____

Hebrews 12:2-3 (NIV)

"Fixing our eyes on Jesus, the pioneer and perfecter of faith. For the joy set before him he endured the cross, scorning its shame, and sat down at the right hand of the throne of God."

_____
_____
_____

Romans 5:5 (NIV)

"And hope does not put us to shame, because God's love has been poured out into our hearts through the Holy Spirit, who has been given to us."

_____
_____
_____

Proverbs 11:2 (NIV)

"When pride comes, then comes disgrace, but with humility comes wisdom."

_____
_____
_____

Proverbs 12:16 (NIV)
"Fools show their annoyance at once, but the prudent overlook an insult."

_____
_____
_____

Ephesians 5:11-12 (NIV)
"Have nothing to do with the fruitless deeds of darkness, but rather expose them. It is shameful even to mention what the disobedient do in secret."

_____
_____
_____

I John 2:28 (NIV)
"And now, dear children, continue in him, so that when he appears we may be confident and unashamed before him at his coming."

_____
_____
_____

II Timothy 2:15 (NIV)
"Do your best to present yourself to God as one approved, a worker who does not need to be ashamed and who correctly handles the word of truth."

Hebrews 12:2 (NIV)
"Fixing our eyes on Jesus, the pioneer and perfecter of faith. For the joy set before him he endured the cross, scorning its shame, and sat down at the right hand of the throne of God."

Daniel 12:2 (NIV)
"Multitudes who sleep in the dust of the earth will awake: some to everlasting life, others to shame and everlasting contempt."

Psalm 71:1 (NIV)
"In you, LORD, I have taken refuge; let me never be put to shame."

I Corinthians 1:27 (NIV)
"But God chose the foolish things of the world to shame the wise; God chose the weak things of the world to shame the strong."

_____
_____
_____

Jeremiah 8:9 (NIV)
"The wise will be put to shame; they will be dismayed and trapped. Since they have rejected the word of the LORD, what kind of wisdom do they have?"

_____
_____
_____

II Kings 2:17 (NIV)
"But they persisted until he was too embarrassed to refuse. So he said, 'Send them.' And they sent fifty men, who searched for three days but did not find him."

_____
_____
_____

II Kings 8:11 (NIV)
"He stared at him with a fixed gaze until Hazael was embarrassed. Then the man of God began to weep."

II Corinthians 7:14 (NIV)
"I had boasted to him about you, and you have not embarrassed me. But just as everything we said to you was true, so our boasting about you to Titus has proved to be true as well."

Personal Reflection

Recall a time when you committed an act and felt shameful and embarrassed about it. Write the details of the incident, how old you were, and how you felt at the time the event transpired.

_____
_____
_____
_____
_____
_____
_____
_____
_____
_____
_____
_____
_____
_____
_____
_____
_____
_____
_____
_____

Were you able to eventually rid yourself of the shame you felt, or do you still carry it today? If you were able to release yourself of the shame, how did you do it? If you continue to experience shame, what can you do to eliminate it from your life?

_____
_____
_____
_____
_____
_____
_____
_____
_____
_____
_____
_____
_____
_____
_____
_____
_____
_____
_____
_____

Group Discussion

Read the following account regarding Isaiah and his commission into the service of the Lord.

Isaiah 6:1-8 (NIV):
> *In the year that King Uzziah died, I saw the Lord, high and exalted, seated on a throne; and the train of his robe filled the temple. ² Above him were seraphim, each with six wings: With two wings they covered their faces, with two they covered their feet, and with two they were flying. ³ And they were calling to one another: "Holy, holy, holy is the LORD Almighty; the whole earth is full of his glory." ⁴ At the sound of their voices the doorposts and thresholds shook and the temple was filled with smoke. ⁵ "Woe to me!" I cried. "I am ruined! For I am a man of unclean lips, and I live among a people of unclean lips, and my eyes have seen the King, the LORD Almighty." ⁶ Then one of the seraphim flew to me with a live coal in his hand, which he had taken with tongs from the altar. ⁷ With it he touched my mouth and said, "See, this has touched your lips; your guilt is taken away and your sin atoned for." ⁸ Then I heard the voice of the Lord saying, "Whom shall I send? And who will go for us?" And I said, "Here am I. Send me!"*

When Isaiah witnessed the presence of the Lord, he was caught off guard because he felt as though he was unworthy. How did the seraphim deal with Isaiah's unclean lips? What does this tell you about a situation you may have been involved in and felt shame? Can God still use you after a sinful or ungodly encounter?

Notes from group discussion:

_____

_____

Living Life **WITHOUT A MASK** Authentically & Unapologetically You!

Regret

Regret is the emotion of wishing one had made a different decision in the past, because the consequences of the decision were unfavorable. Regret is related to perceived opportunity. Its intensity varies over time after the decision, in regard to action versus inaction, and in regard to self-control at a particular age. The self-recrimination which comes with regret is thought to spur corrective action and adaptation.

Viewing regret through a Christian lens:
The Bible refers to regret as a way for Satan to get inside you mentally. Regret can be devastating if you don't keep it in check. I urge you to live with no regrets but look forward for your reward is coming, and there will be nothing to compare with that day but for those who have not yet repented of their sins, which means they have never turned away and forsaken them, there is only a fearful expectation of the coming wrath of God (Hebrews 10:27) that will lead to an ultimate regret for time without end (Revelation 20:12-15). Note- For those who have repented of any wrongdoings, you can look forward to your reward because your sins will be covered by the blood of Jesus. Therefore, you will have nothing to regret.

Use these Bible verses for a better understanding of regret. Read each verse. Then, rewrite it in your own words. Doing so will assist in understanding the concept of regret better.

Genesis 6:7 (NIV)
"So the LORD said, 'I will wipe from the face of the earth the human race I have created—and with them the animals, the birds and the creatures that move along the ground—for I regret that I have made them'."

Living Life **WITHOUT A MASK** Authentically & Unapologetically You!

_____
_____
_____

I Samuel 15:11 (NIV)
"'I regret that I have made Saul king, because he has turned away from me and has not carried out my instructions.' Samuel was angry, and he cried out to the LORD all that night."

_____
_____
_____

II Chronicles 21:20 (NIV)
"Jehoram was thirty-two years old when he became king, and he reigned in Jerusalem eight years. He passed away, to no one's regret, and was buried in the City of David, but not in the tombs of the kings."

_____
_____
_____

II Corinthians 7:8 (NIV)
"Even if I caused you sorrow by my letter, I do not regret it. Though I did regret it—I see that my letter hurt you, but only for a little while."

_____
_____
_____

II Corinthians 7:10 (NIV)

"Godly sorrow brings repentance that leads to salvation and leaves no regret, but worldly sorrow brings death."

Personal Reflection

Most people have done something or said something they regret. Think of a time when you wished you would have done something differently or not acted at all or remained quiet. Why did you regret your actions or words?

_____
_____
_____
_____
_____
_____
_____
_____
_____
_____
_____
_____
_____
_____
_____
_____
_____
_____
_____
_____
_____

Group Discussion

Read these two accounts regarding the results of the regret Judas Iscariot experienced after his betrayal of Jesus.

Acts 1:15-18 (NIV)
> *In those days Peter stood up among the believers (a group numbering about a hundred and twenty) [16] and said, "Brothers and sisters, the Scripture had to be fulfilled in which the Holy Spirit spoke long ago through David concerning Judas, who served as guide for those who arrested Jesus. [17] He was one of our number and shared in our ministry." [18] (With the payment he received for his wickedness, Judas bought a field; there he fell headlong, his body burst open and all his intestines spilled out. [19] Everyone in Jerusalem heard about this, so they called that field in their language Akeldama, that is, Field of Blood.)*

Matthew 27:5 (NIV)
> *So Judas threw the money into the temple and left. Then he went away and hanged himself.*

Judas committed an act against the Lord Jesus, and afterward, he suffered regret. His deep seeded regret caused him to commit suicide. Discuss the serious impacts of regret and why this emotion is important to address.

Notes from group discussion:

_____

_____

_____

Living Life **WITHOUT A MASK** Authentically & Unapologetically You!

Disappointment

Disappointment is the feeling of dissatisfaction that follows the failure of expectations or hopes (State Home and Training School, 1932) to manifest. Similar to regret, it differs in that a person who feels regret focuses primarily on the personal choices that contributed to a poor outcome, while a person feeling disappointment focuses on the outcome itself (Bell, 1985). It is a source of psychological stress (Ma, 2004). The study of disappointment—its causes, impact, and the degree to which individual decisions are motivated by a desire to avoid it—is a focus in the field of decision analysis, (Bell, 1985; van Dijk, Zeelenberg & van der Pligt, 2003) as disappointment is, along with regret, one of two primary emotions involved in decision-making (Van Dijk & Zeelenberg, 2002).

Viewing disappointment through a Christian lens:

Disappointments come in many packages. Job loss, broken relationships, financial insecurity, disappointments within your church community, and the list goes on. One thing you can be sure about is that Jesus understands disappointments. He had disciples who betrayed him to His enemies. He had people who didn't understand or believe Him. He healed people who took Him for granted. Disappointment is part of life, but you don't have to let it rule your life. Trusting in God helps your roots go deep and your ability to withstand trials and disappointments is strengthened by God. God is working on your life. He has started a good work and will not abandon you when the wind shifts or disappointment comes crashing down. In the midst of disappointment, know God is listening and hears your cries. Take that as a comfort. He will always hear you, whether you are happy, sad, heartbroken, or disappointed.

Use these Bible verses for a better understanding of disappointment. Read each verse. Then, rewrite it in your own words. Doing so will assist in understanding the concept of disappointment better.

Job 6:20 (NIV)
"They are distressed, because they had been confident; they arrive there, only to be disappointed."

Isaiah 49:23 (NIV)
"Kings will be your foster fathers, and their queens your nursing mothers. They will bow down before you with their faces to the ground; they will lick the dust at your feet. Then you will know that I am the Lord; those who hope in me will not be disappointed."

Jeremiah 2:36 (NIV)
"Why do you go about so much, changing your ways? You will be disappointed by Egypt as you were by Assyria."

Job 6:20 (NIV)
"They are distressed, because they had been confident; they arrive there, only to be disappointed."

Isaiah 49:23 (NIV)
"Kings will be your foster fathers, and their queens your nursing mothers. They will bow down before you with their faces to the ground; they will lick the dust at your feet. Then you will know that I am the LORD; those who hope in me will not be disappointed."

Jeremiah 2:36 (NIV)
"Why do you go about so much, changing your ways? You will be disappointed by Egypt as you were by Assyria."

John 14:27 (NIV)
"Peace I leave with you; my peace I give you, I do not give to you as the world gives. Do not let your hearts be troubled and do not be afraid."

Psalm 18:3 (NIV)
"In my distress I called to the Lord; I cried to my God for help. From his temple he heard my voice; my cry came before him into his ears."

Personal Reflection

Life is full of disappointments, and they occur unexpectedly. Depending on the depth of the disappointment, they can be difficult to endure, while at other times disappointments can be brushed off easier.

Reflect on a time when you were rather disappointed. What occurred, and why were you disappointed with the situation?

_____
_____
_____
_____
_____
_____
_____
_____
_____
_____
_____
_____
_____
_____
_____
_____
_____
_____
_____
_____

Were your expectations unrealistic or were your thoughts not correctly aligned with the situation? What role did you play (if any) in the disappointment you experienced?

_____
_____
_____
_____
_____
_____
_____
_____
_____
_____
_____
_____
_____
_____
_____
_____
_____
_____
_____
_____
_____

Group Discussion
Read the account of Hannah's disappointment and the results.

I Samuel 1:1-18 (NIV)

> *There was a certain man from Ramathaim, a Zuphite from the hill country of Ephraim, whose name was Elkanah son of Jeroham, the son of Elihu, the son of Tohu, the son of Zuph, an Ephraimite. ² He had two wives; one was called Hannah and the other Peninnah. Peninnah had children, but Hannah had none. ³ Year after year this man went up from his town to worship and sacrifice to the LORD Almighty at Shiloh, where Hophni and Phinehas, the two sons of Eli, were priests of the LORD. ⁴ Whenever the day came for Elkanah to sacrifice, he would give portions of the meat to his wife Peninnah and to all her sons and daughters. ⁵ But to Hannah he gave a double portion because he loved her, and the LORD had closed her womb. ⁶ Because the LORD had closed Hannah's womb, her rival kept provoking her in order to irritate her. ⁷ This went on year after year. Whenever Hannah went up to the house of the LORD, her rival provoked her till she wept and would not eat. ⁸ Her husband Elkanah would say to her, "Hannah, why are you weeping? Why don't you eat? Why are you downhearted? Don't I mean more to you than ten sons?" ⁹ Once when they had finished eating and drinking in Shiloh, Hannah stood up. Now Eli the priest was sitting on his chair by the doorpost of the LORD's house. ¹⁰ In her deep anguish Hannah prayed to the LORD, weeping bitterly. ¹¹ And she made a vow, saying, "LORD Almighty, if you will only look on your servant's misery and remember me, and not forget your servant but give her a son, then I will give him to the LORD for all the days of his life, and no razor will ever be used on his head." ¹² As she kept on praying to the LORD, Eli observed her mouth. ¹³ Hannah was praying in her heart, and her lips were moving but her voice was not heard. Eli thought she was drunk ¹⁴ and said to her, "How long are you going to stay drunk? Put away your wine." ¹⁵ "Not so, my*

lord," Hannah replied, "I am a woman who is deeply troubled. I have not been drinking wine or beer; I was pouring out my soul to the Lord. [16] Do not take your servant for a wicked woman; I have been praying here out of my great anguish and grief." [17] Eli answered, "Go in peace, and may the God of Israel grant you what you have asked of him." [18] She said, "May your servant find favor in your eyes." Then she went her way and ate something, and her face was no longer downcast. [19] Early the next morning they arose and worshiped before the LORD and then went back to their home at Ramah. Elkanah made love to his wife Hannah, and the LORD remembered her. [20] So in the course of time Hannah became pregnant and gave birth to a son. She named him Samuel, saying, "Because I asked the LORD for him."

Discuss how Hannah's disappointment with being barren led her to react in a positive way. What was the end result of the entire matter? What can you learn from Hannah?

Notes from group discussion:

_____

_____

_____

_____

_____

_____

_____

_____

Iniquity
(hidden and unconfessed sin)

Iniquity is moral injustice, wickedness, or sin.

Viewing iniquity through a Christian lens:
Iniquity is a violation of the right or duty that mankind is under obligation to do in accordance with God's Word. An iniquity can also be a wicked act and immoral conduct or practice. These are harmful and offensive to society and especially to God. In the Bible, the terms "sin" and "iniquity" are often used interchangeably.

Use these Bible verses for a better understanding of iniquity. Read each verse. Then, rewrite it in your own words. Doing so will assist in understanding the concept of iniquity better.

Psalm 25:11 (NIV)
"For the sake of your name, LORD, forgive my iniquity, though it is great."

_____

_____

_____

Psalm 32:5 (NIV)
"Then I acknowledged my sin to you and did not cover up my iniquity. I said, 'I will confess my transgressions to the LORD.' And you forgave the guilt of my sin."

Psalm 38:18 (NIV)
"I confess my iniquity; I am troubled by my sin."

Psalm 51:2 (NIV)
"Wash away all my iniquity and cleanse me from my sin."

Psalm 51:9 (NIV)
"Hide your face from my sins and blot out all my iniquity."

Psalm 73:7 (NIV)
"From their callous hearts comes iniquity; their evil imaginations have no limits."

Psalm 85:2 (NIV)
"You forgave the iniquity of your people and covered all their sins."

Psalm 89:32 (NIV)
"I will punish their sin with the rod, their iniquity with flogging."

Psalm 109:14 (NIV)
"May the iniquity of his fathers be remembered before the LORD; may the sin of his mother never be blotted out."

Isaiah 53:6 (NIV)
"We all, like sheep, have gone astray, each of us has turned to our own way; and the LORD has laid on him the iniquity of us all."

Hosea 12:8 (NIV)
"Ephraim boasts, 'I am very rich; I have become wealthy. With all my wealth they will not find in me any iniquity or sin'."

Micah 2:1 (NIV)
"Woe to those who plan iniquity, to those who plot evil on their beds! At morning's light they carry it out because it is in their power to do it."

Zechariah 5:6 (NIV)
"I asked, 'What is it?' He replied, 'It is a basket.' And he added, 'This is the iniquity of the people throughout the land'."

Personal Reflection

Can you recall a time when you committed an atrocity towards God? Share the details below and then reflect. Do you know if God has dealt with you yet? Remember, while some consequences are immediate, others are not. Galatians 6:7-8 (NIV) says, *"Do not be deceived: God cannot be mocked. A man reaps what he sows. ⁸ Whoever sows to please their flesh, from the flesh will reap destruction; whoever sows to please the Spirit, from the Spirit will reap eternal life."*

_____
_____
_____
_____
_____
_____
_____
_____
_____
_____
_____
_____
_____
_____
_____
_____
_____
_____
_____

Dr. C. White-Elliott

Group Discussion
Read the account of Achan and his iniquity and the resulting consequences.

Joshua Chapter 7 (NIV)
> *But the Israelites were unfaithful in regard to the devoted things; Achan son of Karmi, the son of Zimri, the son of Zerah, of the tribe of Judah, took some of them. So the LORD's anger burned against Israel. ² Now Joshua sent men from Jericho to Ai, which is near Beth Aven to the east of Bethel, and told them, "Go up and spy out the region." So the men went up and spied out Ai. ³ When they returned to Joshua, they said, "Not all the army will have to go up against Ai. Send two or three thousand men to take it and do not weary the whole army, for only a few people live there." ⁴ So about three thousand went up; but they were routed by the men of Ai, ⁵ who killed about thirty-six of them. They chased the Israelites from the city gate as far as the stone quarries and struck them down on the slopes. At this the hearts of the people melted in fear and became like water. ⁶ Then Joshua tore his clothes and fell facedown to the ground before the ark of the LORD, remaining there till evening. The elders of Israel did the same, and sprinkled dust on their heads. ⁷ And Joshua said, "Alas, Sovereign LORD, why did you ever bring this people across the Jordan to deliver us into the hands of the Amorites to destroy us? If only we had been content to stay on the other side of the Jordan! ⁸ Pardon your servant, Lord. What can I say, now that Israel has been routed by its enemies? ⁹ The Canaanites and the other people of the country will hear about this and they will surround us and wipe out our name from the earth. What then will you do for your own great name?" ¹⁰ The LORD said to Joshua, "Stand up! What are you doing down on your face? ¹¹ Israel has sinned; they have violated my covenant, which I commanded them to keep. They have taken some of the devoted things; they have stolen, they have lied, they have put*

them with their own possessions. ¹² *That is why the Israelites cannot stand against their enemies; they turn their backs and run because they have been made liable to destruction. I will not be with you anymore unless you destroy whatever among you is devoted to destruction.* ¹³ *"Go, consecrate the people. Tell them, 'Consecrate yourselves in preparation for tomorrow; for this is what the LORD, the God of Israel, says: There are devoted things among you, Israel. You cannot stand against your enemies until you remove them.* ¹⁴ *"'In the morning, present yourselves tribe by tribe. The tribe the LORD chooses shall come forward clan by clan; the clan the LORD chooses shall come forward family by family; and the family the LORD chooses shall come forward man by man.* ¹⁵ *Whoever is caught with the devoted things shall be destroyed by fire, along with all that belongs to him. He has violated the covenant of the LORD and has done an outrageous thing in Israel!'"* ¹⁶ *Early the next morning Joshua had Israel come forward by tribes, and Judah was chosen.* ¹⁷ *The clans of Judah came forward, and the Zerahites were chosen. He had the clan of the Zerahites come forward by families, and Zimri was chosen.* ¹⁸ *Joshua had his family come forward man by man, and Achan son of Karmi, the son of Zimri, the son of Zerah, of the tribe of Judah, was chosen.* ¹⁹ *Then Joshua said to Achan, "My son, give glory to the LORD, the God of Israel, and honor him. Tell me what you have done; do not hide it from me."* ²⁰ *Achan replied, "It is true! I have sinned against the LORD, the God of Israel. This is what I have done:* ²¹ *When I saw in the plunder a beautiful robe from Babylonia, two hundred shekels of silver and a bar of gold weighing fifty shekels, I coveted them and took them. They are hidden in the ground inside my tent, with the silver underneath."* ²² *So Joshua sent messengers, and they ran to the tent, and there it was, hidden in his tent, with the silver underneath.* ²³ *They took the things from the tent, brought them to Joshua and all the Israelites and spread them out before the LORD. ²⁴ Then Joshua, together with all Israel, took Achan son of Zerah, the silver, the robe, the gold bar, his sons and daughters, his cattle, donkeys and sheep, his tent and all that he had, to the Valley of Achor. ²⁵ Joshua said, "Why have you brought this trouble on us? The LORD will bring trouble on you today." Then all Israel stoned him, and after they had stoned the rest, they burned them. ²⁶ Over Achan they heaped up a large pile of rocks, which remains to this day. Then the LORD turned from his fierce anger. Therefore that place has been called the Valley of Achor ever since.*

Notice how Achan's iniquity did not only impact his life; it impacted the life of his entire family and the life of a nation. What is God's perspective on iniquity, and what is the outcome of unconfessed and unrepented sin? Romans 6:26 says, *"For the wages of sin is death; but the gift of God is eternal life through Jesus Christ our Lord."*

Notes from group discussion:

_____
_____
_____
_____
_____
_____
_____
_____

Living Life **WITHOUT A MASK** Authentically & Unapologetically You!

Jealousy

Jealousy generally refers to the thoughts or feelings of insecurity, fear, and concern over a relative lack of possessions or safety. Jealousy can consist of one or more emotions, such as anger, resentment, inadequacy, helplessness, or disgust.

Viewing jealousy through a Christian lens:

The passion of peculiar uneasiness, which arises from the fear that a rival may rob one of the affections of one whom he/she loves, or the suspicion that he/she has already done it; or it is the uneasiness which arises from the fear that another does or will enjoy some advantage which one desires for him/herself. A man's jealousy is excited by the attentions of a rival to his favorite lady. A woman's jealousy is roused by her husband's attentions to another woman. The candidate for office manifests a jealousy of others who seek the same office. In short, jealousy is awakened by whatever may exalt others or give them pleasures and advantages which one desires for him/herself. Jealousy is nearly allied to envy, for jealousy, before a good is lost by ourselves, is converted into envy, after it is obtained by others. Jealousy is the apprehension of superiority. Whoever had qualities to alarm one's jealousy had excellence to deserve one's fondness. It is suspicious fear or apprehension. God's jealousy signifies His concern for His own character and government, with a holy indignation against those who violate His laws, and offend against His majesty (Psalm 79) ("Jealousy," *King James Dictionary Definition*, 2023).

Use these Bible verses for a better understanding of jealousy. Read each verse. Then, rewrite it in your own words. Doing so will assist in understanding the concept of jealousy better.

Genesis 30:1 (NIV)
"When Rachel saw that she was not bearing Jacob any children, she became jealous of her sister. So she said to Jacob, 'Give me children, or I'll die!'"

_____
_____
_____

Genesis 37:11 (NIV)
"His brothers were jealous of him, but his father kept the matter in mind."

_____
_____
_____

Exodus 20:5 (NIV)
"You shall not bow down to them or worship them; for I, the LORD your God, am a jealous God, punishing the children for the sin of the parents to the third and fourth generation of those who hate me."

_____
_____
_____

Numbers 11:29 (NIV)
"But Moses replied, "Are you jealous for my sake? I wish that all the LORD's people were prophets and that the LORD would put his Spirit on them!"

Deuteronomy 32:16 (NIV)
"They made him jealous with their foreign gods and angered him with their detestable idols."

I Kings 14:22 (NIV)
"Judah did evil in the eyes of the LORD. By the sins they committed they stirred up his jealous anger more than those who were before them had done."

Isaiah 11:13 (NIV)
"Ephraim's jealousy will vanish, and Judah's enemies will be destroyed; Ephraim will not be jealous of Judah, nor Judah hostile toward Ephraim."

Ezekiel 16:42 (NIV)
"Then my wrath against you will subside and my jealous anger will turn away from you; I will be calm and no longer angry."

_____
_____
_____

Zechariah 1:14 (NIV)
"Then the angel who was speaking to me said, Proclaim this word: This is what the LORD Almighty says: I am very jealous for Jerusalem and Zion."

_____
_____
_____

Acts 7:9 (NIV)
"Because the patriarchs were jealous of Joseph, they sold him as a slave into Egypt. But God was with him."

_____
_____
_____

Personal Reflection

Recall a time when you experienced jealousy. What were you jealous about? After you experienced jealousy, what did you do next? What feeling came afterward? What would you recommend to friends and family about having a jealous spirit?

Group Discussion

Read the following account of Rachel and Leah. Who was jealous and why? How was the situation resolved?

Genesis 30:1-24 (NIV)

> *When Rachel saw that she was not bearing Jacob any children, she became jealous of her sister. So she said to Jacob, "Give me children, or I'll die!" ² Jacob became angry with her and said, "Am I in the place of God, who has kept you from having children?" ³ Then she said, "Here is Bilhah, my servant. Sleep with her so that she can bear children for me and I too can build a family through her." ⁴ So she gave him her servant Bilhah as a wife. Jacob slept with her, ⁵ and she became pregnant and bore him a son. ⁶ Then Rachel said, "God has vindicated me; he has listened to my plea and given me a son." Because of this she named him Dan. ⁷ Rachel's servant Bilhah conceived again and bore Jacob a second son. ⁸ Then Rachel said, "I have had a great struggle with my sister, and I have won." So she named him Naphtali. ⁹ When Leah saw that she had stopped having children, she took her servant Zilpah and gave her to Jacob as a wife. ¹⁰ Leah's servant Zilpah bore Jacob a son. ¹¹ Then Leah said, "What good fortune!" So she named him Gad. ¹² Leah's servant Zilpah bore Jacob a second son. ¹³ Then Leah said, "How happy I am! The women will call me happy." So she named him Asher. ¹⁴ During wheat harvest, Reuben went out into the fields and found some mandrake plants, which he brought to his mother Leah. Rachel said to Leah, "Please give me some of your son's mandrakes." ¹⁵ But she said to her, "Wasn't it enough that you took away my husband? Will you take my son's mandrakes too?" "Very well," Rachel said, "he can sleep with you tonight in return for your son's mandrakes." ¹⁶ So when Jacob came in from the fields that evening, Leah went out to meet him. "You must sleep with me," she said. "I have hired you with my son's mandrakes." So he slept*

with her that night. ⁱ⁷God listened to Leah, and she became pregnant and bore Jacob a fifth son. ¹⁸Then Leah said, "God has rewarded me for giving my servant to my husband." So she named him Issachar. ¹⁹Leah conceived again and bore Jacob a sixth son. ²⁰Then Leah said, "God has presented me with a precious gift. This time my husband will treat me with honor, because I have borne him six sons." So she named him Zebulun. ²¹Some time later she gave birth to a daughter and named her Dinah. ²²Then God remembered Rachel; he listened to her and enabled her to conceive. ²³She became pregnant and gave birth to a son and said, "God has taken away my disgrace." ²⁴She named him Joseph, and said, "May the LORD add to me another son."

Notes from group discussion:

_____
_____
_____
_____
_____
_____
_____
_____
_____
_____
_____

Living Life **WITHOUT A MASK** Authentically & Unapologetically You!

Envy

Envy is an emotion which occurs when a person lacks another's quality, skill, achievement, or possession and either desires it or wishes that the other lacked it (Parrott & Smith, 1993). Aristotle defined envy as pain at the sight of another's good fortune, stirred by "those who have what we ought to have" ("Rhetoric," Aristotle, 2023). Bertrand Russell (1930) said envy was one of the most potent causes of unhappiness. Recent research considered the conditions under which it occurs, how people deal with it, and whether it can inspire people to emulate those they envy (Duffy, Lee & Adair, 2021).

Viewing envy through a Christian lens:

Sin of jealousy over the blessings and achievements of others, especially the spiritual enjoyment and advancement of the kingdom of Christ freely and graciously bestowed upon the people of God. Envy manifests the insidiousness of sin and human depravity apart from the intervention of God's redeeming grace. As a sin of the flesh, envy characterizes the lives of the unregenerate. Envy is one of the traits of the Christian's former way of life (Romans 13:8-14; Titus 3:3). Those who practice envy and strife are barred from the kingdom of heaven (Galatians 5:19-26). Indeed, the unregenerate nature ever tends toward envy, manifesting the unbeliever's rejection of God, His truth, and His will for human conduct (James 3:14, 16).

Use these Bible verses for a better understanding of envy. Read each verse. Then, rewrite it in your own words. Doing so will assist in understanding the concept of envy better.

Job 5:2 (NIV)
"Resentment kills a fool, and envy slays the simple."

Proverbs 3:31 (NIV)
"Do not envy the violent or choose any of their ways."

Proverbs 14:30 (NIV)
"A heart at peace gives life to the body, but envy rots the bones."

Proverbs 23:17 (NIV)
"Do not let your heart envy sinners, but always be zealous for the fear of the LORD."

Proverbs 24:1 (NIV)
"Do not envy the wicked, do not desire their company."

Ecclesiastes 4:4 (NIV)
"And I saw that all toil and all achievement spring from one person's envy of another. This too is meaningless, a chasing after the wind."

I Corinthians 13:4 (NIV)
"Love is patient, love is kind. It does not envy, it does not boast, it is not proud."

Galatians 5:21 (NIV)
"...and envy; drunkenness, orgies, and the like. I warn you, as I did before, that those who live like this will not inherit the kingdom of God."

Philippians 1:15 (NIV)
"It is true that some preach Christ out of envy and rivalry, but others out of goodwill."

_____

_____

_____

Titus 3:3 (NIV)
"At one time we too were foolish, disobedient, deceived and enslaved by all kinds of passions and pleasures. We lived in malice and envy, being hated and hating one another."

_____

_____

_____

James 3:14 (NIV)
"But if you harbor bitter envy and selfish ambition in your hearts, do not boast about it or deny the truth."

_____

_____

_____

James 3:16 (NIV)
"For where you have envy and selfish ambition, there you find disorder and every evil practice."

Dr. C. White-Elliott

_____

_____

_____

I Peter 2:1 (NIV)
"Therefore, rid yourselves of all malice and all deceit, hypocrisy, envy, and slander of every kind."

_____

_____

_____

Personal Reflection

Have you ever experienced the green-eyed monster of envy? What was the occasion? How did you handle it?

_____
_____
_____
_____
_____
_____
_____
_____
_____
_____
_____
_____
_____
_____
_____
_____
_____
_____
_____
_____
_____
_____
_____

Looking back at your reaction, how could have you responded differently?

Group Discussion

Read the following account of how some react while walking in the spirit of envy. Notice how God can cause a negative emotion to have a positive outcome. However, there may not be an associated earthly or heavenly reward attached to it.

Philippians 1:15-18 (NIV):

It is true that some preach Christ out of envy and rivalry, but others out of goodwill. 16 The latter do so out of love, knowing that I am put here for the defense of the gospel. 17 The former preach Christ out of selfish ambition, not sincerely, supposing that they can stir up trouble for me while I am in chains. 18 But what does it matter? The important thing is that in every way, whether from false motives or true, Christ is preached. And because of this I rejoice.

Notes from group discussion:

_____
_____
_____
_____
_____
_____
_____
_____
_____
_____

Dr. C. White-Elliott

Covetousness
(greed)

Covetousness/greed is an insatiable desire for material gain (be it food, money, land, or animate/inanimate possessions) or social value, such as status, position, or power. Greed has been identified as undesirable throughout known human history because it creates behavior-conflict between personal and social goals.

Viewing covetousness through a Christian lens:
Strong desire to have that which belongs to another. It is considered to be a very grievous offense in Scripture. The tenth commandment forbids coveting anything that belongs to a neighbor, including his house, his wife, his servants, his ox or donkey, or anything that belongs to him (Exodus 20:17). Jesus listed covetousness or greed along with many of the sins from within, including adultery, theft, and murder, which make a person unclean (Mark 7:22). Paul reminded the Ephesians that greed or covetousness is equated with immorality and impurity, so that these must be put away (Ephesians 5:3). A covetous or greedy person is an idolator (5:5) and covetousness is idolatry (Colossians 3:5). James warns that people kill and covet because they cannot have what they want (4:2).

Covetousness, therefore, is basic to the commandments against murder, adultery, stealing, and lying. Those who accept bribes are coveting, leading to murder (Ezekiel 22:12). Coveting a neighbor's wife is a form of adultery (Exodus 20:17). Achan admitted to coveting a robe and silver and gold, so he stole them, which was a sin against the Lord (Joshua 7:20-22). Gehazi, the servant of Elisha, coveted the property of Naaman so much that he lied to get what he wanted from Naaman the leper (II Kings 5:19-25) and was struck with leprosy. Proverbs warns that a covetous person brings trouble to his family (15:27). Thus, covetousness is the root of all kinds of sins, so Jesus gave the warning, *"Be on your guard against all kinds of greed"* (Luke 12:15) ("Covetousness," *Baker's Evangelical Dictionary of Biblical Theology*, 2023).

Use these Bible verses for a better understanding of covetousness. Read each verse. Then, rewrite it in your own words. Doing so will assist in understanding the concept of covetousness better.

Exodus 20:17 (NIV)
"You shall not covet your neighbor's house. You shall not covet your neighbor's wife, or his male or female servant, his ox or donkey, or anything that belongs to your neighbor."

_____

_____

_____

Exodus 34:24 (NIV)
"I will drive out nations before you and enlarge your territory, and no one will covet your land when you go up three times each year to appear before the LORD your God."

_____

_____

_____

Deuteronomy 7:25 (NIV)
"The images of their gods you are to burn in the fire. Do not covet the silver and gold on them, and do not take it for yourselves, or you will be ensnared by it, for it is detestable to the LORD your God."

_____

_____

_____

Micah 2:2 (NIV)
"They covet fields and seize them, and houses, and take them. They defraud people of their homes, they rob them of their inheritance."

_____
_____
_____

Romans 7:7 (NIV)
"What shall we say, then? Is the law sinful? Certainly not! Nevertheless, I would not have known what sin was had it not been for the law. For I would not have known what coveting really was if the law had not said, 'You shall not covet'."

_____
_____
_____

Romans 13:9 (NIV)
"The commandments, 'You shall not commit adultery,' 'You shall not murder,' 'You shall not steal,' 'You shall not covet,' and whatever other command there may be, are summed up in this one command: 'Love your neighbor as yourself'."

_____
_____
_____

James 4:2 (NIV)
"You desire but do not have, so you kill. You covet but you cannot get what you want, so you quarrel and fight. You do not have because you do not ask God."

Personal Reflection

Share an account when you looked upon someone and coveted what the person had, such as a talent, a possession, or even a personality or physical trait. Did your covetous spirit change your disposition toward the person? How so?

_____
_____
_____
_____
_____
_____
_____
_____
_____
_____
_____
_____
_____
_____
_____
_____
_____
_____
_____
_____

Dr. C. White-Elliott

Group Discussion

Read the following account of King Saul. Notice how the spirit of covetousness can cause one to walk in the spirit of disobedience.

I Samuel 15:1-9 (NIV)
> *Samuel said to Saul, "I am the one the L*ORD *sent to anoint you king over his people Israel; so listen now to the message from the L*ORD*. ² This is what the L*ORD *Almighty says: 'I will punish the Amalekites for what they did to Israel when they waylaid them as they came up from Egypt. ³ Now go, attack the Amalekites and totally destroy all that belongs to them. Do not spare them; put to death men and women, children and infants, cattle and sheep, camels and donkeys.'" ⁴ So Saul summoned the men and mustered them at Telaim—two hundred thousand foot soldiers and ten thousand from Judah. ⁵ Saul went to the city of Amalek and set an ambush in the ravine. ⁶ Then he said to the Kenites, "Go away, leave the Amalekites so that I do not destroy you along with them; for you showed kindness to all the Israelites when they came up out of Egypt." So the Kenites moved away from the Amalekites. ⁷ Then Saul attacked the Amalekites all the way from Havilah to Shur, near the eastern border of Egypt. ⁸ He took Agag king of the Amalekites alive, and all his people he totally destroyed with the sword. ⁹ But Saul and the army spared Agag and the best of the sheep and cattle, the fat calves and lambs—everything that was good. These they were unwilling to destroy completely, but everything that was despised and weak they totally destroyed.*

Notes from group discussion:

_____

_____

Living Life **WITHOUT A MASK** Authentically & Unapologetically You!

Chapter Three
Remove the Mask

Chapter Three
Remove the Mask

After completing all of the exercises in Chapters One and Two, you have identified the characteristics that currently comprise your personality, those you are lacking but desire to attain, and those you desire to eliminate.

Now, it is time to work to remove any masks you may wear, so you can bring yourself one step closer to living as your authentic self. In doing so, you will find renewed security, stability, and a sense of worth as you work to experience pure joy.

Why be Authentic?

It is not always easy to live authentically. At times, being true to who you are may mean going against the crowd. It may mean being unconventional, opening yourself up for the possibility of others hurting you, and taking the harder road.

On one hand, it may mean missing some opportunities to engage with different groups of people. This is something you will have to accept. However, in the longer term, being authentic is likely to open up many more opportunities, opportunities that simply would not be available to someone who has been seen to be shifty, conflicted, vacillating, or inauthentic.

Living an authentic life is also vastly more rewarding than hiding your true self. When you live authentically, you will have less concern about what you said (or did not say), how you acted, or whether you did the right thing. Living authentically means you can trust yourself and your motivations implicitly. However, it does not remove complete concern about those circumstances. After all, our actions, reactions, and words are always cause for concern, but living according to our own principles will cause us to second guess ourselves less frequently.

There are several other benefits of being authentic.

Trust and respect: When you are true to yourself, you not only trust the judgments and decisions you make, but others trust you as well. They will respect you for standing by your values and beliefs.

Personal Reflection

Do you currently find that people trust and respect you for your opinions, ideas, and perspectives?

_____

_____

_____

What makes you believe they do or do not? What do they do or say?

_____

_____

_____

_____

How does their outlook of you as a trustworthy and respectable person feel?

_____

_____

_____

Integrity: When you are authentic, you also have integrity because when you are honest with yourself, you can be honest with others. Furthermore, you do not hesitate to do the right thing, so you never have to second-guess yourself. Who you are, what you do, and what you believe in should align perfectly.

Personal Reflection
Viewing yourself from the outside, do you believe your friends, family, and colleagues consider you to be a person of integrity? Why or why not?

_____
_____
_____
_____
_____
_____
_____
_____
_____

Ability to deal with problems: When you are honest with yourself and others, you have the strength and openness to deal with problems quickly instead of procrastinating or ignoring them altogether.

Personal Reflection
When you are faced with an issue, what is your immediate response? Do you begin to logically assess the situation? Do you have an emotional reaction? Do you immediately consult others for guidance?

Do other people come to you with their problems? If so, why? If no one comes to you regarding their concerns, what do you think the reasons are?

Realizing potential: When you trust yourself and do what you know is right, you can realize your full potential in life. Instead of letting others dictate what is best for you, you take control of your life.

Personal Reflection
Do you realize the potential you embody? How do you realize it?

_____
_____
_____
_____
_____
_____
_____
_____
_____
_____
_____

Do you allow others to lead you into the next phase of your life, or do you determine the next phase on your own?

_____
_____
_____
_____
_____
_____

Confidence and self-esteem: You can trust yourself to make the right decisions when you are being genuine and doing the right thing. In turn, this leads to higher self-confidence and self-esteem, greater optimism, and more life satisfaction.

Personal Reflection

Rate your level of confidence and self-esteem on a scale from 1 to 10, with 10 being the highest ranking. Explain the reason for your ranking.

Less stress: How would you feel if, every day, you said what you meant, stayed true to yourself, and behaved accordingly? Imagine the joy and self-respect you would feel! Being authentic is far less stressful than being someone you are not.

Personal Reflection

Describe how your life would be different if you exercised and experienced the eight traits listed above (trust, respect, integrity, facing problems, potential, confidence, self-esteem, and reduced stress).

_____
_____
_____
_____
_____
_____
_____
_____
_____
_____
_____
_____
_____
_____
_____
_____
_____
_____

Note: *Honesty is an important part of authenticity. However, there's a distinct difference between being brutally honest and being truthful with others. We should always strive to be truthful with those around us, because others sometimes view brutal honesty as aggressive, judgmental, or even arrogant. Uncensored honesty can also jeopardize our relationships and careers.*

Being Authentic in Different Roles

If you are like most people, you may have a number of different identities at work and in your personal life. For instance, you are a leader to your team, a co-worker or friend to your colleagues, a team member to your boss, and an expert to your clients. Do you have to act the same in each role in order to be authentic? It is an important question, especially because many of us seem to have seemingly conflicting "selves." So, we need to be flexible, and this flexibility can allow us to change, grow, and realize new opportunities. However, our true self remains the same no matter what situation we are in. Just because we have different roles to play does not mean we have to wear different masks along the way.

How to Be Authentic

You will not find and develop your authentic self overnight. Rather, it is a lifelong process of discovery. Take the following steps to begin:

1. *Live by Your Values*

Most people consciously (and for the rest unconsciously) adopt a moral code (a set of values and beliefs) for their life. For some, it is based on the societal code that is propagated by the society in which they are surrounded. For others, it is the moral code taught by family members, namely parents. And for others, it is a spiritual or religious code, they have adopted for their life.

Living authentically means first, living according to the values and beliefs you hold dear, and second, the personal goals you pursue emerge from your values and beliefs. Your first step is to identify your core values, and then to commit to living and working according to them. You then need to set personal goals and career goals that align with these. Sometimes, you might have to make an ethically challenging decision; this is when knowing your core values will help you do the right thing.

Personal Reflection
Have you set core values for your life? What are they based upon?

_____
_____
_____
_____
_____
_____
_____

Does everyone in your immediate circle share the same values? If not, how do they differ?

_____
_____
_____
_____
_____

Do these differences present challenges within the group? If so, how?

2. *Identify the Gap*

Is there a gap between who you are now and the person you desire to be? For instance, do you put on a mask when you are at work? Perhaps, you are more abrasive with your team than you would like to be because you think that is how a leader gets things done. Maybe you adopt a flippant attitude because you don't want others to think you are boring because you take a serious attitude to your job. Or, maybe you are brimming with ideas that you never share because you are afraid your team will shoot them down, and that leaves you feeling stifled and unhappy.

Revisit the three lists of characteristics you composed at the beginning of Chapter One. Choose one word from the second list that you want to start working on. For instance, perhaps you want to be more "open." Resolve to work on this every day. It is more realistic to set small goals and work on one trait at a time than it is to try to transform your entire life all at once.

Personal Reflection

Take the characteristics from the second list at the beginning of Chapter One, and place them in the order you plan to work on them. If the characteristics are listed within this book, use the corresponding scriptures to assist in your development of that trait. If the trait is not covered in this book, use a Bible concordance to find related Bible verses to assist you.

1. _____
2. _____
3. _____
4. _____
5. _____
6. _____
7. _____
8. _____
9. _____
10. _____

3. *Live with Integrity*

It takes courage to develop and preserve integrity. Start by analyzing the daily choices you make. You will often intuitively know what the right and wrong choices are. Your goal is to learn how to listen to that "small voice" – that sense of unease – that tells you something is wrong. The still, small voice is the voice of the Holy Spirit who is guiding you. Study each choice you make, and ask yourself which one will make you feel good about yourself the next day.

Please note- the spirit of complacency will block your sense of what is right. That spirit will need to be eradicated prior to moving forward. Living with integrity also means you take responsibility for your actions, including your mistakes. Own up to the choices you make, and work tirelessly to right any shortcomings.

Personal Reflection
Read the following account of Joseph and Potiphar's wife.

Genesis Chapter 38 (NIV)
> Now Joseph had been taken down to Egypt. Potiphar, an Egyptian who was one of Pharaoh's officials, the captain of the guard, bought him from the Ishmaelites who had taken him there. ² The LORD was with Joseph so that he prospered, and he lived in the house of his Egyptian master. ³ When his master saw that the LORD was with him and that the LORD gave him success in everything he did, ⁴ Joseph found favor in his eyes and became his attendant. Potiphar put him in charge of his household, and he entrusted to his care everything he owned. ⁵ From the time he put him in charge of his household and of all that he owned, the LORD blessed the household of the Egyptian because of Joseph. The blessing of the LORD was on everything Potiphar had, both in the house and in the field. ⁶ So Potiphar left everything he had in Joseph's care; with Joseph in charge, he did not concern himself with anything except the food he ate. Now Joseph was well-built and handsome, ⁷ and after a while his master's wife took notice of Joseph and said, "Come to bed with me!" ⁸ But he refused. "With me in charge," he told her, "my master does not concern himself with anything in the house; everything he owns he has entrusted to my care. ⁹ No one is greater in this house than I am. My master has withheld nothing from me except you, because you are his wife. How then could I do such a wicked thing and sin against God?" ¹⁰ And though she spoke to Joseph day after day, he refused to go to bed with her or even be with her. ¹¹ One day he went into the house to attend to his

duties, and none of the household servants was inside. ¹² *She caught him by his cloak and said, "Come to bed with me!" But he left his cloak in her hand and ran out of the house.* ¹³ *When she saw that he had left his cloak in her hand and had run out of the house,* ¹⁴ *she called her household servants. "Look," she said to them, "this Hebrew has been brought to us to make sport of us! He came in here to sleep with me, but I screamed.* ¹⁵ *When he heard me scream for help, he left his cloak beside me and ran out of the house."* ¹⁶ *She kept his cloak beside her until his master came home.* ¹⁷ *Then she told him this story: "That Hebrew slave you brought us came to me to make sport of me.* ¹⁸ *But as soon as I screamed for help, he left his cloak beside me and ran out of the house."* ¹⁹ *When his master heard the story his wife told him, saying, "This is how your slave treated me," he burned with anger.* ²⁰ *Joseph's master took him and put him in prison, the place where the king's prisoners were confined. But while Joseph was there in the prison,* ²¹ *the LORD was with him; he showed him kindness and granted him favor in the eyes of the prison warden.* ²² *So the warden put Joseph in charge of all those held in the prison, and he was made responsible for all that was done there.* ²³ *The warden paid no attention to anything under Joseph's care, because the LORD was with Joseph and gave him success in whatever he did.*

What would you have done if you were in Joseph's situation when his master's wife propositioned you?

_____
_____
_____
_____
_____

Group Discussion

After reading the account of Joseph and Potiphar's wife, discuss the possible outcomes that may have resulted if Joseph had yielded to temptation.

Notes from group discussion:

4. *Communicate Honestly*

Honest communication involves saying what you mean, while respecting other people's needs and feelings. This takes emotional intelligence and good communication skills. It also means not playing games. Speak your mind in a clear manner, and do not rely on cryptic hints or other tactics to get your point across. Communicating honestly also means keeping your promises. If you give your word to someone, then treat it as a bond. Never make a promise you cannot keep. In the event, you are unable to keep your word, share the change with the person immediately and not after the fact. Not holding true to your word can cause a break down in a relationship that may prove difficult to repair.

Personal Reflection

Recall a time when someone made a commitment to you and then broke the commitment without prior warning. Also, share the feelings the incident caused you to have.

_____
_____
_____
_____
_____
_____
_____
_____
_____
_____

Share a time when you made a commitment to someone and did not follow through. How did you handle the situation? How did the person(s) respond? How did you feel?

Group Discussion

Share various emotions that may arise when someone does not hold to his/her end of a commitment? Discuss methods for dealing with commitments in an effort to honor one's word. Also, discuss how commitments should be dealt with if one cannot follow through.

Notes from group discussion:

Dr. C. White-Elliott

5. Don't Make Assumptions

It is easy to go through life making assumptions about others. When judgment is not strictly necessary, try your best to suspend your judgments. Let others' actions speak for themselves, and try to take their words at face value. When the person's actions are unclear, engage him/her in dialogue, giving the person an opportunity to explain him/herself rather than assuming the worst. You might find that as you make an effort to be open-minded with others, they will extend the same courtesy to you. Isn't that what we all desire?

Personal Reflection

Share a time when someone made an assumption about you. Was the assumption accurate? How did the assumption make you feel?

_____
_____
_____
_____
_____
_____
_____

Share an occasion when you made an assumption about someone else that turned out to be false. What was the final outcome?

_____
_____
_____

Group Discussion

Read the account of two sisters: Mary and Martha. Discuss the assumption Martha made about her sister Mary and Jesus' response. What can we learn about assumptions?

Luke 10:38-41 (NIV)

> As Jesus and his disciples were on their way, he came to a village where a woman named Martha opened her home to him. [39] She had a sister called Mary, who sat at the Lord's feet listening to what he said. [40] But Martha was distracted by all the preparations that had to be made. She came to him and asked, "Lord, don't you care that my sister has left me to do the work by myself? Tell her to help me!" [41] "Martha, Martha," the Lord answered, "you are worried and upset about many things, [42] but few things are needed—or indeed only one. Mary has chosen what is better, and it will not be taken away from her."

Notes from group discussion:

Living Life **WITHOUT A MASK** Authentically & Unapologetically You!

6. *Develop Self-Confidence*

Authenticity requires strength of character, especially when others are pressuring you to act in a way you know is wrong. This is why you should work on building your self-confidence. A strong sense of self and the assertiveness needed to stand your ground will help you get through challenging situations.

Personal Reflection

How would you rate your current level of self-confidence on a scale of 1-10, with 10 being the highest rating? Explain your rationale for your rating.

_____
_____
_____
_____
_____
_____
_____

Do you know someone who embodies a high level of self-esteem? What indicators have you detected that caused you to make that assessment?

_____
_____
_____
_____
_____

Living Life **WITHOUT A MASK** Authentically & Unapologetically You!

_____

_____

_____

Group Discussion

Read the account of Moses at the burning bush when he was commissioned by God to return to Egypt and speak to Pharoah on behalf of God regarding God's chosen people, the Israelites. What is Moses' disposition towards God's instructions? How would you have responded if you were in Moses' position?

Exodus Chapter 3 (NIV)

> *Now Moses was tending the flock of Jethro his father-in-law, the priest of Midian, and he led the flock to the far side of the wilderness and came to Horeb, the mountain of God. ² There the angel of the LORD appeared to him in flames of fire from within a bush. Moses saw that though the bush was on fire it did not burn up. ³ So Moses thought, "I will go over and see this strange sight— why the bush does not burn up." ⁴ When the LORD saw that he had gone over to look, God called to him from within the bush, "Moses! Moses!" And Moses said, "Here I am." ⁵ "Do not come any closer," God said. "Take off your sandals, for the place where you are standing is holy ground." ⁶ Then he said, "I am the God of your father, the God of Abraham, the God of Isaac and the God of Jacob." At this, Moses hid his face, because he was afraid to look at God. ⁷ The LORD said, "I have indeed seen the misery of my people in Egypt. I have heard them crying out because of their slave drivers, and I am concerned about their suffering. ⁸ So I have come down to rescue them from the hand of the Egyptians and to bring them up out of that land into a good and spacious land, a land*

flowing with milk and honey—the home of the Canaanites, Hittites, Amorites, Perizzites, Hivites and Jebusites. [9] And now the cry of the Israelites has reached me, and I have seen the way the Egyptians are oppressing them. [10] So now, go. I am sending you to Pharaoh to bring my people the Israelites out of Egypt." [11] But Moses said to God, "Who am I that I should go to Pharaoh and bring the Israelites out of Egypt?" [12] And God said, "I will be with you. And this will be the sign to you that it is I who have sent you: When you have brought the people out of Egypt, you will worship God on this mountain." [13] Moses said to God, "Suppose I go to the Israelites and say to them, 'The God of your fathers has sent me to you,' and they ask me, 'What is his name?' Then what shall I tell them?" [14] God said to Moses, "I AM WHO I AM. This is what you are to say to the Israelites: 'I AM has sent me to you.'" [15] God also said to Moses, "Say to the Israelites, 'The LORD, the God of your fathers—the God of Abraham, the God of Isaac and the God of Jacob—has sent me to you.' "This is my name forever, the name you shall call me from generation to generation. [16] "Go, assemble the elders of Israel and say to them, 'The LORD, the God of your fathers—the God of Abraham, Isaac and Jacob—appeared to me and said: I have watched over you and have seen what has been done to you in Egypt. [17] And I have promised to bring you up out of your misery in Egypt into the land of the Canaanites, Hittites, Amorites, Perizzites, Hivites and Jebusites—a land flowing with milk and honey.' [18] "The elders of Israel will listen to you. Then you and the elders are to go to the king of Egypt and say to him, 'The LORD, the God of the Hebrews, has met with us. Let us take a three-day journey into the wilderness to offer sacrifices to the LORD our God.' [19] But I know that the king of Egypt will not let you go unless a mighty hand compels him. [20] So I will stretch out my hand and strike the Egyptians with all the wonders that I will perform among them. After that, he will let you go. [21] "And I will make the Egyptians favorably disposed toward this people, so that when you leave you will not go empty-handed. ²² Every woman is to ask her neighbor and any woman living in her house for articles of silver and gold and for clothing, which you will put on your sons and daughters. And so you will plunder the Egyptians."

Notes from group discussion:

_____
_____
_____
_____
_____
_____
_____
_____
_____
_____
_____
_____
_____
_____
_____
_____
_____
_____

7. *Manage Your Emotions*

When you live authentically, you consider others' needs, and you do your best to treat them with courtesy and respect. In stressful situations, this means knowing how to control your emotions. This is an important part of living authentically, because it shows you have inner strength and respect for those around you, and it is a skill worth developing as it will serve you well in all aspects of your life and career.

Personal Reflection

Have you ever flown off the handle and said or did something you later regretted? Share one account and provide details of the incident and your response.

How did the other involved party respond to your reaction?

Looking back in retrospect, how could you have reacted differently?

Would a different reaction have provided a different outcome? Why or why not?

Group Discussion

Read the result of the first plague the Lord sent upon Egypt when Pharoah refused to respond positively to God's appeal. What could have been possible outcomes if Pharoah's response had been different?

Exodus 7:14-24 (NIV)

> *Then the L*ORD *said to Moses, "Pharaoh's heart is unyielding; he refuses to let the people go. ¹⁵ Go to Pharaoh in the morning as he goes out to the river. Confront him on the bank of the Nile, and take in your hand the staff that was changed into a snake. ¹⁶ Then say to him, 'The L*ORD*, the God of the Hebrews, has sent me to say to you: Let my people go, so that they may worship me in the wilderness. But until now you have not listened. ¹⁷ This is what the L*ORD *says: By this you will know that I am the L*ORD*: With the staff that is in my hand I will strike the water of the Nile, and it will be changed into blood. ¹⁸ The fish in the Nile will die, and the river will stink; the Egyptians will not be able to drink its water.'" ¹⁹ The L*ORD *said to Moses, "Tell Aaron, 'Take your staff and stretch out your hand over the waters of Egypt—over the streams and canals, over the ponds and all the reservoirs—and they will turn to blood.' Blood will be everywhere in Egypt, even in vessels of wood and stone." ²⁰ Moses and Aaron did just as the L*ORD *had commanded. He raised his staff in the presence of Pharaoh and his officials and struck the water of the Nile, and all the water was changed into blood. ²¹ The fish in the Nile died, and the river smelled so bad that the Egyptians could not drink its water. Blood was everywhere in Egypt. ²² But the Egyptian magicians did the same things by their secret arts, and Pharaoh's heart became hard; he would not listen to Moses and Aaron, just as the L*ORD *had said. ²³ Instead, he turned and went into his palace, and did not take even this to heart. ²⁴ And all the Egyptians dug along the Nile to get drinking water, because they could not drink the water of the river.*

Dr. C. White-Elliott

Notes from group discussion:

Chapter Four
Developing Self Assuredness

Chapter Four
Developing Self-Assuredness

Dealing with Insecurities and the Fear of Judgment

We are often called a narcissistic generation. We are told that technology and social media are giving us an inflated sense of self. But most of us do not walk around feeling like we are all that great. In fact, there is one underlying emotion that overwhelmingly shapes our self-image and influences our behavior, and that is insecurity, which was discussed at length in Chapter Two. If you could enter the minds of people around you, even the narcissistic ones, you are likely to encounter ceaseless waves of insecurity. A recent survey found that 60 percent of women experience hurtful, self-critical thoughts on a weekly basis.

The most common self-critical thought people have toward themselves is that they are different – not in a positive sense, but in some negative, alienating way. Whether our self-esteem is high or low, one thing is clear; we are a generation that compares, evaluates and judges ourselves with great scrutiny. By understanding where this insecurity comes from, why we are driven to put ourselves down and how this viewpoint affects us, we can start to challenge and overcome the destructive inner critic that limits our lives.

Insecurity can affect us in countless areas of our lives. Every person will notice his/her inner critic being more vocal in one area or another. For example, you may feel pretty confident at work but completely lost in your love life or vice versa. You may even notice that when one area improves, the other deteriorates. Most of us can relate, at one time or another, to having self-sabotaging thoughts toward ourselves about our career or other important aspects of our life. Old feelings that we are incompetent or that we will never be acknowledged or appreciated can send our insecurities through the roof.

Whether we are single, dating or in a serious, long-term relationship, there are many ways our critical inner voice can creep in to our romantic lives. Relationships, in particular, can stir up past hurts and experiences. They can awaken insecurities we have long buried and bring up emotions we do not expect. Moreover, many of us harbor unconscious fears of intimacy. Being close to someone can shake us up and bring these emotions and critical inner voices even closer to the surface. Listening to this inner critic can do serious damage to our interpersonal relationships. It can cause us to feel desperate toward our partner or pull back when things start to get serious. It can exaggerate feelings of jealousy or possessiveness or leave us feeling rejected and unworthy.

Here are eleven ways to deal with insecurity and replace it with self-assuredness, which is self-acceptance coupled with confidence. One particular method may be best for you or a combination of methods may be the solution for you to employ.

1. *Talk to a Spiritual Counselor*

Just as you would not try to set your broken bone or remove your gallbladder, so don't try to resolve your insecurities if they require professional care. Counselors can provide the most effective and efficient form of treatments to establish long periods of well-being and security. To locate a qualified counselor, begin at your local church. There are many ministers and elders who are skilled in offering godly counsel. Counselors may be able to provide you with tools you can use to maintain balanced levels of mental and emotional security.

Personal Reflection

Do you have any preconditioned concerns about seeing a counselor? If so, why?

Have you ever had any sessions with a counselor? If so, did you reap any benefits?

Did you find in order to see a counselor a specific state of mind was required? Why?

Would you be open to scheduling an initial session with a counselor?

Are there any concerns you have about whether or not the counselor can lead you in the right direction? If so, what is the cause of your concerns?

_____
_____
_____
_____
_____
_____
_____
_____

2. *Acknowledge the Role of Insecurity in Daily Life*

With insecurity, it can feel that the problem is only there part of the time or that it does not affect your life in any significant ways. These views could be true, but it is invaluable to take an honest look at your life and ask yourself how insecurity influences your school, work, trust, communication, self-esteem, and mental health.

Personal Reflection

In which areas have insecurities been demonstrated in your life?

_____
_____
_____
_____
_____
_____
_____
_____
_____

What has been your best method for dealing with insecurities? Do these methods always help?

_____
_____
_____
_____
_____
_____
_____
_____

What emotions have you found to be attached to insecurities? How do you deal with those emotions?

_____
_____
_____
_____
_____
_____
_____
_____

3. *Fully Assess the Source of Insecurity*

When people are insecure, it can feel like outside issues, situations, and people are causing the problems. Surely outside forces play a role in insecurity, but it is up to the individual to address the root problem. As insecurity rises from past life experiences, mental health issues, or current relationships, be sure to plan interventions that target the source. Take an honest assessment of the root cause by taking note of when the feeling of insecurity arises. What happened directly prior? Once we have a better sense of where our insecurities emanate and the profound influence it has on our lives, we can begin to change it. We can start by interrupting the critical inner voice process, the one that repeats the falsehood in our mind.

Personal Reflection

Recall a time when you felt extremely insecure. What was the catalyst for the emotion? What can you do to circumvent the effects of the catalyst?

_____
_____
_____
_____
_____
_____
_____
_____

4. *Practice Unconditional Self-Compassion*

When insecurity is the issue, you will need tremendous amounts of compassion and self-love. Rather than seeking these from others, you will create more change by giving them to yourself. Loving yourself creates more security within yourself. To exhibit self-love to yourself, turn the negative thoughts into positive statements. For example, if someone has told you that you will never have a healthy love relationship, turn it around by saying, "I will have a healthy love relationship. God will heal this relationship and turn the negativity around, or God will give me someone who will love me for me without tearing me down."

Also, speak the Word of God into and over your life. For example, say, "Lord, you said in your Word, in Malachi 3:11, that you would rebuke the devourer for my sake. The enemy is trying to devour my mind and my emotions. Father, rebuke him for my sake."

Personal Reflection

Recall a statement someone said to you or an action someone performed that impacted your level of security. Write it here, and then, rewrite the statement/action as a statement/action of affirmation, one that uplifts you and gives you hope, peace, and feelings of love. Complete this exercise a few times until you get the hang of it. Use extra paper if needed.

Statement/Action One-

_____
_____
_____
_____

Statement/Action Rewritten-

_____
_____

Living Life **WITHOUT A MASK** Authentically & Unapologetically You!

_____
_____

Statement/Action Two-

_____
_____
_____
_____

Statement/Action Rewritten-

_____
_____
_____
_____

Statement/Action Three-

_____
_____
_____
_____

Statement/Action Rewritten-

Group Discussion
How did it feel to turn the negative statements or actions into positive ones?

Notes from group discussion:

_____

_____

_____

_____

_____

5. *Retrain Yourself*

Many early lessons and examples people around you demonstrated in your early years along with the experiences you have today all contribute to your insecurities. Taking a long look at your beliefs about yourself, other people, and the world around you can teach yourself new views. However, as people of God, reading and hearing the Word of God will have the greatest impact on shaping your view. Through this process, you can establish security and self-worth.

Personal Reflection

How often do you hear, read, and meditate on God's Word?

_____

_____

_____

_____

How long have you been studying God's Word? (Over what duration of time, i.e. five years, six months, etc.)

_____

_____

Have you noticed a difference in your viewpoints from then to now? Explain.

Group Discussion
Share the impacts the Word of God has had in your life.

Notes from group discussion:

_____
_____
_____
_____
_____
_____
_____

6. Openly Communicate Your Insecurity Concerns

Insecurity makes people unsure and uncertain about relationships, causing them to be uncomfortable sharing their experiences and feelings with others, but this approach only breeds isolation and shame. A lack of communication can harm your relationship, so take the opposite approach by being open with trusted supporters about what you endure and what they can do to help. Be sure to keep your expectations realistic. Do not expect too much from others to the point you become reliant upon them. That can lead to dependency issues. Express your insecurities to your loved ones, mental health provider, and physical health provider.

Personal Reflection

Everyone should have a circle of supporters. The number of individuals within that circle is irrelevant. Within your circle of supporters, hopefully you feel comfortable enough to share your insecurities. Can you think of at least two individuals with whom you can share? Write their names below. Schedule a time to sit down with the individuals and open yourself up for dialogue. After you do so, write your experiences here. Share how you feel before, during, and after the conversation.

Dr. C. White-Elliott

Person 1- _____

Experience:

_____
_____
_____
_____
_____
_____
_____

Person 2- _____

Experience:

_____
_____
_____
_____
_____
_____
_____

List the names of the individuals in your core group of supporters.

1. _____
2. _____
3. _____
4. _____
5. _____

Group Discussion
Share how you felt when you engaged in dialogue with the two individuals from your circle of supporters. If you were not able to embark upon this adventure, take time to listen intently to what others in the group have to say about their experiences. Maybe what they share will motivate you to take the leap toward opening up.

Notes from group discussion:

_____
_____
_____
_____
_____
_____
_____
_____
_____

_____
_____
_____
_____
_____
_____

7. Build a Strong Support Network

You will always need a strong group of people in your corner. Having healthy, happy friends and loved ones around you will help to further shift your perspectives from the views you have held. They can expose you to new places, people, and experiences that will build your confidence as well.

Personal Reflection

After option six, maybe you found your group of supporters was inadequate, and maybe you did not really feel comfortable sharing with anyone in your current network. If that is the case, take steps to add others to your support group. As you go through seasons in your life, you will find your group of supporters will shift. Some individuals will drop out of your group while others will be added in. Take the time to notice who is around you and who has become dependable during this season of your life.

Make a list of individuals who may be added to the group of supporters you listed for option six.

1. _____
2. _____
3. _____
4. _____
5. _____

8. *Focus on the Positives*

The way you talk to yourself and the way you see the world will have a major impact on your insecurities. People who speak to themselves more positively, challenge their negative self-talk, stay focused on the future, and find good things in the world around them tend to be more secure and comfortable. These may feel like foreign concepts initially, but they pay off in the long term.

Personal Reflection

Now it is time to do a little research. Search the Internet for six quotes or affirmations you can speak into your own life on a daily basis to assist with having a positive outlook. Even if the affirmation seems a bit far-fetched, if it makes you joyful and peaceful, add it to your list. You might also want to include a few Bible verses within this list that will offer you encouragement as well.

List the quotes, affirmations, and Bible verses here:

1. _____
   _____
2. _____
   _____
3. _____
   _____
4. _____
   _____
5. _____
   _____

Group Discussion

Share your list of affirmations with the group, and if you hear any positive affirmations from the group members that you find encouraging, add them to your list.

Notes from group discussion:

_____
_____
_____
_____
_____
_____
_____
_____
_____
_____
_____
_____
_____
_____
_____
_____
_____
_____
_____
_____

9. Take Care of Your Physical Health

Exercising, getting good sleep, and eating healthier foods will help lower mental health symptoms and improve self-esteem. When people are physically healthier, they tend to be mentally healthier, so start with small changes and build consistency over time.

Personal Reflection

Make a list of four characteristics you would like to change about your physical self. Rank them in the order of least challenging to most challenging. Then, develop a short-term or long-term plan for dealing with the four characteristics, depending upon the severity of overcoming them.

1. _____

2. _____

3. _____

4. _____

Group Discussion

Share one item from your list of four and the plan you have developed for overcoming that particular characteristic.

Notes from group discussion:

_____

_____

10. *Accept Your Limitations & Celebrate Your Differences*

Change is good, and moving in new directions can help people accomplish great things. The problems arise when people become fixated on changing the unchangeable. Accept what you cannot change and find peace with your insecurities. Find ways to embrace what makes you uncomfortable.

Personal Reflection

Recite the Serenity Prayer every day for the next week until it gets into your spirit. If you need more time to grasp the point that your power and authority are limited, add on another week.

"God, grant me the serenity to accept the things I cannot change, the courage to change the things I can, and the wisdom to know the difference."
Serenity Prayer by Reinhold Niebuhr

11. *Aim for Progress, Not Perfection*

Feeling perfectly secure at all times is not possible. There is no such state as perfection, so aim for progress. Look at where you have come, where you are, and where you are going. Appreciate your path and stay committed to change.

Personal Reflection

Look back over the last five years of your life and assess the progress you have made with your self-development. Note the changes here.

_____
_____
_____
_____
_____
_____
_____

Dr. C. White-Elliott

_____

_____

_____

Final Thoughts on Insecurity

Insecurity is a universal experience, but not all people experience insecurity so intensely that it disrupts their life and ability to function. If insecurity is creating unwanted impacts in your mental, social, or physical health, it could be time to take action and address the issue with professional support and assistance.

Here are four ways to stop living in fear of judgment:
1. Nothing lasts forever. The reality is that the human brain has limited data reserves. Although we may make judgments, they are not significant enough to earn a place in our memory banks for eternity. So when someone makes a judgment about you, chances are that moments or days later that judgment will have left his/her conscious awareness. The same is true with us. The only reason we remember their judgments is because we choose to. We can actually forget their judgments by chalking them up to nonfactors. The reality though is those who are closest to us have a greater impact on us, and their words can cut like a knife. Those judgments are more difficult to forget, but it is not impossible.

2. Judgment is unavoidable. Stop trying to control the judgments of others. It has become part of our persona to demand that others not judge us. Think about popular statements such as, "No judgments" and "This is a non-judgment zone." None of this really helps because you cannot control what others think. Maybe they won't express their judgment, but it does not mean

they can stop a physiological brain process. Judging is a normal human behavior.

3. Let them judge! It can be liberating in an intimate relationship to just allow judgments to be present. Instead of stopping yourself from being open or vulnerable or from sharing something negative but important about yourself, do it anyway. Remind yourself that close and intimate relationships deepen when people risk judgment. If this openness does not happen, it does not necessarily mean you have done something wrong, but it may mean the person you are working to connect with does not have the capacity for an emotionally intimate relationship.

4. Notice your own judgments. There is no better way to care less about the judgments of others than to judge yourself more and others less. Of course, judgment is unavoidable, but watch the language you use in your own head about the people and events in your life. Do not judge others too harshly. Give them grace to be human. At the same time, do not judge yourself too harshly. Give yourself grace to be human. Remember, to err is human!

With all you have read, studied and worked through, you are growing and developing into a more assured person who embodies the full confidence to walk in your authenticity. Do not allow anyone to rob you of the strong, healthy, loving person you are who can tackle what comes your way without crumbling or succumbing to the ways of the world. Stand tall and assume your right to maintain and present your uniqueness as you glorify and honor the Lord Jesus!

References

Aristotle. "Rhetoric." (2023). Classics at MIT. Translated by Roberts, W. Rhys. MIT.

Bell, David E. (January 1985). "Putting a premium on regret." *Management Science.* **31***(1)*: 117-20.

"Contentment: What it is and Why it Matters." *Clarity Clinic.* (2020).

"Dedication." Oxford Dictionary. (2023).

"Definition of integrity in English." *Oxford Living Dictionaries.* (2023). Oxford University Press.

Duffy, Michelle K.; Lee, KiYoung; Adair, Elizabeth A. (21 January 2021). "Workplace Envy". *Annual Review of Organizational Psychology and Organizational Behavior.* **8***(1)*: 19-44.

"Embarrassment." *Psychology Today.*

Grossmann, I. (2017). "Wisdom in context." *Perspectives on Psychological Science.* **21***(12)*: 1254–1266.

"Humble." Wiktionary.com. (2023).

"Intelligence." Encyclopedia Britannica. (2023).

"Jealousy." 2023. King James Dictionary Definition.

Killinger, Barbara. (2010). *Integrity: Doing the Right Thing for the Right Reason.* McGill-Queen's University Press. p. 12.

Lancelot, Tucker. (2022). "What is the Story of Job?" christianity.com.

Lancer, D. (2014). *Conquering Shame and Codependency: 8 Steps to Freeing the True You.* Hazelden Foundation, pp. 12–13.

Lopez, Shane J., ed. (2009). "Compassion". *Encyclopedia of Positive Psychology.* Malden, MA: Wiley-Blackwell.

Lucaites, John Louis; Condit, Celeste Michelle; Caudill, Sally (1999). *Contemporary rhetorical theory: a reader.* Guilford Press. p. 92.

Ma, Lybi. (2004-03-29). "Down But Not Out." *Psychology Today.*

MacCallum, Gerald Cushing (1993). Legislative Intent and Other Essays on Law, Politics, and Morality. Univ. of Wisconsin Press. p. 152.

"Meaning of integrity in English." *Cambridge Dictionary.* (2023). Cambridge University Press.

Parrott, W. G.; Smith, R. H. (1993). "Distinguishing the experiences of envy and jealousy." *Journal of Personality and Social Psychology.* **64***(6)*: 906–920.

Parsa, S. (2018). "Psychological Construction of Shame in Disordered Eating." *New Psychology Bulletin*, **15***(1)*, 11–19.

Patterson, Eric. (2022). choosingtherapy.com.

Pillai, Krishna. (2011). Essence of a Manager. Springer Science & Business Media. p. 163.

Russell, Bertrand. (1930). *The Conquest of Happiness.* NY: H. Liverwright.

Schwarzer, Ralf (2012). *Personality, human development, and culture: international perspectives on psychological science.* Hove: Psychology. pp. 127–129; Greenberg, Jeff; Sander L. Koole; Tom Pyszczynski. (2013). *Handbook of Experimental Existential Psychology.* Guilford Publications. p. 162.

Shein, L. (2018). "The Evolution of Shame and Guilt". PLoSONE, **13***(7)*, 1-11.

Spurgeon, Charles Haddon (1871), *The Fourfold Treasure,* №991.

Snyder, C.R.; Lopez, Shane J. (2001). *Handbook of Positive Psychology.* Oxford University Press. p. 413.

State Home and Training School, Mich, Michigan. Lapeer (1932). *Staff Papers, 1932.* The University of Michigan. p. 31.

Staudinger, U.M. & Glück, J. (2011). "Psychological wisdom research: Commonalities and differences in a growing field." *Annual Review of Psychology.* 62: 215–241.

Strong's Online Concordance. (2023).

Tracy, Jessica; Robins, Richard (2007). "Self-conscious emotions: Where self and emotion meet". In Sedikides, C. (ed.). *Frontiers of social psychology. The self.* Psychology Press. pp. 187–209.

"Wisdom." (2023). *Oxford English Dictionary.*

van Dijk, Wilco W. & Marcel Zeelenberg (December 2002). "Investigating the appraisal patterns of regret and disappointment". *Motivation and Emotion.* **26***(4)*: 321–31.

van Dijk, Wilco W.; Zeelenberg, Marcel; van der Pligt, Joop (2003). "Blessed are those who expect nothing: Lowering expectations as a way of avoiding disappointment." *Journal of Economic Psychology.* 24*(4)*: 505–16.

Walsh, Roger (June 2015). "What Is wisdom? Cross-cultural and cross-disciplinary Syntheses." *Review of General Psychology.* 19*(3)*: 178–293.

"Wisdom." Dictionary.com. (2023).

"Wisdom." *Oxford English Dictionary.* Oxford University Press. (2023).

About the Author

Dr. Cassundra White-Elliott resides in California with her family, where as an English/ Education professor, she teaches at various community colleges.

As an author, she composes with the direction of the Holy Spirit, in an effort to share with God's people all He has for them.

In addition to teaching and writing, Dr. Elliott also serves as an evangelistic teacher. She is also the founder of Int'l Women's Commission, a women's ministry that serves the needs of the entire person, by attending to healing the mind, body, soul, and spirit. Her desire is to empower women everywhere.

Dr. Elliott holds a Ph.D. in Education, a Master's degree in English Composition, and a Bachelor's degree in Education.

Dr. Elliott is the founder and editor-in-chief for *Christian Inspiration* magazine, which covers topics germane to Christian living and the world at large.

Dr. Elliott is also the founder of CLF Publishing Collaborative, LLC. For your publishing needs, go online to www.clfpublishing.org.

Gift of Salvation for Non-Believers

*"For all have sinned, and come
short of the glory of God."*
(Romans 3:23)

This section was written especially for non-believers, those who have not accepted the gift of salvation. The gift of salvation saves souls from eternal damnation and is a free gift offered by God Himself.

John 3:16-18 says, *"For God so loved the world, that he gave his only begotten Son, that whosoever believeth in him should not perish, but have everlasting life. For God sent not his Son into the world to condemn the world; but that the world through him might be saved. He that believeth on him is not condemned: but he that believeth not is condemned already, because he hath not believed in the name of the only begotten Son of God."*

This section of scripture tells us God's purpose for giving His son Jesus to the world. The world was in a bad condition. The world was over-wrought with sin; the people were living for fleshly desires rather than for God's desires.

As a result of the world's conditions, God decided He would offer the perfect sacrifice that would save the world from being a place where people were lost and had no hope. He decided His own son could stand in proxy for the sin-filled world, taking all sin upon Himself.

So, Jesus came, born of a virgin, to save this dying world. He walked on this earth for 33 ½ years, doing the work of His Heavenly Father. At the appointed time, He died by way of crucifixion upon a cross at Calvary, on Golgotha's hill. He shed His blood and died for you and for me. Because His blood was pure, it paid the penalty for all unrighteousness and gave those who believe in Him direct access to His father's throne.

Scripture tells us in Matthew 27:51 that the veil of the temple was ripped in two from top to bottom, at the moment that Jesus' spirit left His body. As a result of the veil's removal, we are no longer required to have a high priest make intercession for us. We, as the children of the Most High God, are able to approach the throne of God for ourselves, and Jesus sits on the right hand of the Father making intercession for us.

But what is even more miraculous than God offering His own son as the perfect sacrifice was the fact that when Jesus was placed in grave clothes and placed in a tomb, He only remained there until the third day. God would not have it that His son would remain in the heart of the earth forever. In order for people to believe in the awesome power of God and His dear son Jesus, a miracle had to be performed. So, on the third day, after Jesus died on the cross, He was resurrected, demonstrating the omnipotence of God. This very act was the act that would cause people to believe in a god that reigns supreme and holds the power of the universe in His very hands, a god that could save them from themselves.

Today, if you are an unbeliever, you can change your destiny. You can change where you will spend your eternity. Our Heavenly Father gives us the freedom of choice about how we want to live our life here on earth and how we want to spend eternity. In Deuteronomy 30:19, God boldly declares, "*I call heaven and earth to record this day against you, that I have set before you life and death, blessing and cursing: therefore choose life, that both thou and thy seed may live."*

So, dear friend what choice will you make today? Will you spend your eternity with the Creator or will you suffer Hell's eternal flames? Again, the choice is yours. Just as the men aboard the ship who were with Jonah became believers, you too can make a choice to accept the only one and true living God as your god.

If after reading the above passages, you have decided that you want to spend your eternity in Heaven with God, the Creator, and His son Jesus, and the Holy Spirit, read through what has affectionately come to be known as the Roman's Road. This is the road to salvation. As you read through the scrip-ures that comprise the Roman's Road, you will also read the explanation for each scripture, so you will have clarity about what you are reading and confessing.

The Roman's Road to Salvation

The road to salvation begins with Romans 3:23 which declares, *"For all have sinned, and come short of the glory of God."* This scripture explains that everyone has come short of God's glory and needs redemption. Then, Romans 6:23a states, *"For the wages of sin is death."* Here, we learn that the consequence of living a life of sin is death. Everyone will experience physical death as a result of the sin committed in the garden of Eden, but those who commit themselves to a life of sin will suffer eternal damnation in the lake of fire (Rev. 19). Continue with the rest of verse 6:23 that says, *"but the gift of God is eternal life through Jesus Christ our Lord."* There is an alternative to suffering eternal damnation. We can accept the gift of salvation by accepting Jesus as our personal Lord and Savior. Then, Romans 5:8 says, *"But God commendeth his love toward us, in that, while we were yet sinners, Christ died for us."* We are able to receive the gift of salvation because Christ came to earth and shed His blood for us on the cross.

Continue to Romans 10: 9-10 which says, *"That if thou shalt confess with thy mouth the Lord Jesus, and shalt believe in thine heart that God hath raised him from the dead, thou shalt be saved. For with the heart man believeth unto righteousness; and with the mouth confession is made unto salvation."* If we confess with our mouths that Jesus is the son of God, that He came and died for our sins, and that God raised Him from the dead, we will receive salvation.

Finish with Romans 10:13, which states, *"For whosoever shall call upon the name of the Lord shall be saved."* Call upon the name of God by saying these words, **"Lord Jesus, come into my heart and save me, Lord. I believe that you are the Son of God who came and died on the cross for my sins. I believe that you rose from the grave. I also believe that you now sit in heaven on the right side of the Father, making intercession for me. I accept you as my Lord and my Savior."**

Now that you have confessed with your mouth that Jesus is the son of God and that He died for our sins and rose from the grave, **YOU ARE NOW SAVED!!!!** You will spend your eternity in heaven.

The next step is very important- you must find a Bible-based church that teaches the Word of God and confesses the Lord Jesus Christ to be the son of God. Don't delay. Do this immediately. Do not leave yourself open to the enemy. Get connected with the saints of the Most High God and keep yourself covered with the unspotted blood of the Lamb.

Here is my prayer for you.
Father God,
I thank you for the opportunity to minister your word to the unsaved, the unchurched, and the uncommitted. Father God, I pray now for the souls who have just received the gift of salvation. Lord Father, they have opened their hearts to you, and I know that you have received them into your kingdom and written their names in the Book of Life. Father God, I pray that you will touch their lives and show yourself mightily before them. Let their eyes be opened by the scales falling off, allowing them to see clearly.

Father God, I even pray for the backslider, those who have turned away from you after receiving the gift of salvation. You said in your Word that you desire that none would perish. So Lord, I send your Word to them right now, praying that they would confess the iniquity in their heart, repent, and turn from their evil ways, so that they may receive a life of abundance. You said in your Word in Matthew Chapter 14, that every knee shall bow before you and every tongue will confess that Jesus is Lord.

Father God, I pray now that we all come under subjection to your Word and that we will humbly submit our lives to you. I ask all these things in the name of my Lord and Savior Jesus Christ.
Amen, Amen, Amen!!!!

I will continue to pray for your success in your walk with God. Remember, this spiritual walk that you are about to embark on will not be an easy walk, but remember, the race is not given to the swift but to those who endure to the end.

Be blessed with heaven's best. I love you!

Additional Titles by the Author

Pub. Speaking in the Spir. (2002)
Do You Know God? (2004)
Unleashed Anger (2005)
Unleashed Anger Daily Prayer (2005)
Two of a Kind (2006)
Dare to Succeed by Breaking Through Barriers (2007)
Dare to Succeed Prayer Guide (2007)
Through the Storm (2007)
Lord, Teach Me to…Blessing! (2007)
The Preacher's Daughter (2007)
The Preacher's Son (2009)
Where is Your Joppa? (2009)
From Despair, through Determination, to Victory! (2009)
Fear Not (2011)
Mayhem in the Hamptons (2012)
After the Dust Settles (2013)
A Mother's Heart (2013)
A Diamond in the Rough (2013)
The Power of a Woman (2013)
365 Days of Encouragement (2013)
A Touch in the Dark (2014)
Broken Chains (2014)
I Have Fallen (2014)
The Bottom Line (2015)
Set Free (2015)
Daughter, God Loves You (2016)
A Mother's Heart II (2016)
Living a Balanced Life (2016)
Kimara & Aaron…Disneyland (2016)
Embracing Womanhood (2017)
A Mother's Heart III (2017)
Web of Lies (2017)
Time is Running Out (2017)
Revisiting Grammar & Business Writing Essentials (2017)
Test Preparation: Writing Essentials, Mathematics Review & Reasoning Skills (2017)
The Making of Dr. C. (2018)
Claim Your Inheritance (2018)
Women's Study Bible New International Version (2018)
Christian Inspiration (2019-present)
Safety in Him (2019)
A Mother's Heart IV (2019)
A is for Adam (2019)
Have You Walked in My Shoes? (2019)
Prepare for Battle (2019)
B is for Babel (2020)
C is for Christ (2020)
D is for David (2020)
E is Eve (2020)
F is for Forgiveness (2020)
G is for Givers (2020)
H is for Helping Others (2020)
I is for Idols (2020)
J is for Joseph (2020)
K is for Kindness (2020)
The Last Shall Be First: An Analysis of the Systemic Subdivide of Black America (2021)
L is for Love (2021)
M is for Mary (2021)
N is for Noah's Ark (2021)
is for Obedience (2021)
Rest in Him: Scriptures for Daily Peace (2021)
P is for Paul the Apostle (2021)
Q is for Queen Esther (2021)
Be Ye Inspired Vol. 1 (2021)
R is for Ruth (2021)
Be Ye Inspired Vol. II (2022)
S is for Samuel (2022)
T is for Truth (2022)
U is for Unconditional Love (2022)
V is for Victory (2022)
W is for Worship (2022)
X is for Xerxes (2022)
Y is for You (2022)
Pearls of Wisdom (2022)
Z is for Zachariah (2022)
Pearls of Wisdom Quotes & Journal (2022)
Shift Your Narrative (2023)